D1314042

CITISTATE SEATTLE

Shaping a Modern Metropolis

Mark L. Hinshaw, AICP, FAIA

PLANNERS PRESS
AMERICAN PLANNING ASSOCIATION
Chicago, Illinois
Washington, D.C.

Cover photos: C. Jacobson
Background photo: Denni Shefrin

Copyright 1999 by the American Planning Association
122 S. Michigan Ave., Suite 1600, Chicago, IL 60603

ISBN (paperback): 1-884829-22-8
ISBN (hardbound): 1-884829-23-6

Library of Congress Catalog Card Number 98-74096

Printed in the United States of America

Contents

Foreword

By Neal Peirce

Bon-bons and urban planning rarely come in a single package. But Mark Hinshaw pulls off the combination, with finesse and fine humor, in this book.

There's not one exhaustive lesson between these covers; it would take daring defiance of academic guild principles to sneak this volume into a classroom. Instead, with droplets of urban observation and wisdom, you find yourself subtly educated in elements and principles of good cities.

And having a wonderful time doing it. What makes the Pike Place Market so fabulous. The magic of old-time movie house architecture. Such gems to discover as the new Port of Seattle building, the ZymoGenetics firm's magical remake of the old City Light Steam Plant, or the artful redesign of the Frye Art Museum into a building beckoning for hours of delight.

Nor is it just design Hinshaw seeks out. There's a little chapter on Seattle's ubiquitous espresso stands. Another on how supermarkets can accommodate themselves to the design fabric of seasoned neighborhoods. And Mon Dieu!—one on potties for pedestrians!

There's another Hinshaw voice to be heard in these pages, especially the ones addressing such topics as zoning's checkered history, tuckaway homes and starter houses, and the "why not?" question of decent and humane design of apartment buildings. It's a voice of sometimes withering critique and appropriate impatience with mediocrity. Enough pin pricks to keep these pages jumping.

The term "citistate," used in the title and through the pages which follow, was invented by my colleague Curtis Johnson and myself to describe the metropolitan regions of today's world. Rather than political boundaries, we see citistate regions as organic, dynamic expressions of how late 20th century humanity comes together for trade, commerce, and communication.

The sleek contraction of the ancient "city-state" term into the one word "citistate" seems to be to reflect characteristics special to our time. Unlike their ancestors of ancient Greece or the Hanseatic League, today's urban regions are at the center of instant global electronic communications, chief transfer points for capital moving across continents and hemispheres, and the lead recipients of world population growth.

Few words, of course, are perfect, and we sometimes worry that "citistate" may carry too heavy an aura of cold globalism, even slick "corporate-speak." Indeed, think of the Seattle region as the headquarters of such world-wide heavyweights as Microsoft and Boeing, and the corporate association of the word "citistate" fits quite well.

But regions are not just global competitors; they are the places we live our lives—we shape them and then they shape us, as Winston Churchill observed. The built environment is desperately important. And why indeed should a flavorful, livable built environment be limited to center cities fortunate enough to have been built a half century or more ago? Can't *the rest* of the citistate look good too? Who says it must give in to mass marketing and engineering tyranny and emerge as a dull ocean of look-alike, mediocre satellite cities and subdivisions?

Mark Hinshaw doesn't think so. And proves it, as with friendly and inquiring eye he looks for, and finds, the urbanity of places well outside Seattle's municipal boundaries. The mini-chapters on Tacoma and Everett are among the most appealing of this book, precisely because Hinshaw can show the character and care with which these major satellites to Seattle are being developed in our time. The same is even true for Bellevue, a community Hinshaw himself helped point towards creation of real urban fabric where there was so little to start with.

He applies the same measure of imagination to *very* new places one associates with minimal planning and maximum commercial clutter. Top example: Tukwila. By the time one's finished reading about its community center complex and then the back-to-basics brilliance of its Foster High School, an overwhelming conclusion emerges: if it can happen in that community, then why not *all* communities within citistate Seattle?

Lots of folks will want this book for their personal pleasure and years of happy weekend explorations. But it could effect even more. Imagine getting it into the hands of the area's high school and college students, of local government officials, businesses, developers, civic movers-and-shakers. There'd have to be a big impact. No city, suburb, neighborhood subdivision would be free of fresh, bottoms-up demand for radically improved planning and design.

After that, all we'll need will be a small battalion of Mark Hinshaws to write companion books for all of America's citistates.

Introduction

By the Honorable Paul Schell
Mayor of the City of Seattle

This is a book about a city and a region I've become deeply attached to over the past 30 years. And it is perfect that the book is built of many little chapters—many pieces: a hidden neighborhood on the Duwamish River, espresso stands, experimental housing, an art museum, the love of a steam plant. This is Seattle—young, gritty, elegant, full of interesting details and disparities. In fact, I'm a disparity myself. Mayor of a city on the crest of the world's technology wave and I can barely use e-mail.

But that's why Seattle is exciting. We really are still a frontier, seat-of-the-pants kind of town, where individuals can make a difference.

Great cities have always been active centers of interchange—of commerce, ideas, culture, art. They've been the sites of ongoing chemical reactions that have had massive effects on our civilization. Venice, London, Vienna, Tokyo, New York—each city, in its own way has been a place where ideas can blossom. I really believe Seattle has all the makings of becoming a truly great city in a style all its own.

Of course Seattle is no Venice. Our art museum is only a few years old and, as I write this, our symphony hall is yet a few weeks from birth. Our transportation system, though more efficient than gondolas, still needs some serious work. But all this is changing. Downtown is full of new construction including a major new center for international trade; our neighborhoods are deep in the process of planning for their own futures; and we've spent enough time in the national and international limelight as the latest "hip," "livable," "best" city that it's starting to seem silly.

We *are* coming of age. And how we handle ourselves during this time of massive growth and maturation is important.

We are no longer a town that can slap up poorly constructed buildings in response to the heat of a momentary market, as we did during the Alaskan gold rush 100 years ago. What we build now we must expect to live with for a long time. And we can no longer afford to think of ourselves as a clean little city surrounded by a permanent and unchanging natural environment. Our presence—our growth—is changing that environment, year by year. Yet we are still young enough, new enough, that well-made decisions can truly shape what happens to our architectural landscape, to our natural environment, and to how this city lives its daily life. We have the failures and successes of other cities to learn from. We have a healthy economy to work with. And we have a population of citizens not so entrenched in what *was* and *is* that they can't get excited by what *can be*.

Back when I was fresh out of law school and looking about for a place to make a start, I chose Seattle because it seemed young and small enough to be a place where a person—even an out-of-towner—could have an impact on the community. It also had the diversity of people, neighborhoods, languages, and economies that made it a real *city* rather than just a big town. That was 30 years ago.

Since that time, as Director of the Department of Community Development, I've been able to help preserve Pike Place Market and Pioneer Square, and carry out the city's first neighborhood improvement program. With Allied Arts, I helped create Seattle's "1 Percent for Arts" program. As a developer, I've worked to revitalize First Avenue while holding onto its history. As Dean of the College of Urban Architecture and Planning I joined in the effort to promote a holistic approach to urban planning as a way to strengthen community. As Port Commissioner I worked on increasing the city's role in international trade. And now, as Mayor, I'm kind of working on it all.

Each one of these roles has given me the chance to get to know a different side of Seattle. And together they've given me a deep appreciation for the complexity of parts that shape what this city is. It is the decisions made by individual citizens, businesses, and organizations—not government—that build the fabric of our community.

Growth and change are exciting, but they are also risky. In times like these, it's easy to lose sight of the details that count—the bits of history and character, the new experiments, and the individual expressions and eccentricities of a person or group that give depth and character to city life. Yet without these bits and pieces we lose our soul. We need them. We need to notice them, talk about them, write about them. I'm glad for this book, and I'm glad for the part Mark plays in getting us to open our eyes, to point and say "Hey, look at that!"

Seattle has the makings of a great city. But if we are going to like ourselves, we need to know who we are. Ultimately, it's all in the details.

Preface

On a hillside northeast of La Conner, Washington, down the road from the tiny hamlet of Bow, a commune called "Equality Colony" was founded a little more than 100 years ago. Though the community long ago disappeared, "Colony Road" still exists as a mute reminder of the turn-of-the-century social experiment. My grandmother was born on that commune.

As family accounts have it, my great-grandparents had lived on the Eastern Seaboard, in an area of the country marked by overcrowded buildings, unsafe working conditions, and drinking water tainted by human and industrial waste.

Jim and Jeannette Brady were taken with reformist writings of the time by Eugene Debs and others. Among the pamphlets that they subscribed to was a call for families who were interested in starting a new community. Out in a far corner of the country, in the new State of Washington, a small group of people had purchased a few dozen acres, set up a sawmill, and were clearing the land for a settlement. The young couple packed up their belongings and set out for a new life in the frontier.

True to their socialist beliefs, the colonists did not build individual log cabins, but rather an interconnected set of dwellings, with a common kitchen and social room. Men and women had equal voting rights, years before the 19th Amendment was ratified. Food, clothing, and other items were produced for all of the residents to share. But, like many other social experiments, the colony's energy and resources eventually dissipated. Disillusioned, my great-grandparents took their young daughter down the coast to California, where most of their children and their children's children were born and where they continue to live.

I never met my great-grandparents, and it is not very likely that genes carry with them a world view. However, for most of my adult life I have been thoroughly fascinated with communities, social movements, and unconventional forms of housing. As an architect and city planner, I have worked with scores of communities, organizations, and individuals proposing ways of making places to live and work safer, more convenient, and more pleasant. I have also written articles that have explored issues in urban design, both for professional journals as well as for local newspapers.

As a writer, it is always great fun to poke at the newest art museum or office building. But it is the buildings out in the neighborhoods, out where we live, that mean the most to us. So, while not ignoring the big things, I have looked particularly for the small things, those heroic efforts by individuals and organizations to respect the landscape and to make this region a better place to live.

Like my great-grandparents almost 100 years ago, I see the Citistate of Seattle as having an ethic, one that tempers an individual, entrepreneurial spirit with a sense of what is best for all of us as a whole. Thankfully, we have buildings, places, and communities that reflect this ethic.

❧❧❧❧

There are a number of people to whom I wish to express gratitude for their assistance in writing this book. Jennifer Donnelly, Catherine Goetz, and Mary McCumber read and commented on drafts. Jennifer also assisted in the references. Karen West at *The Seattle Times* edited my columns for five years with great tact and encouragement. David Brewster, former publisher of *The Seattle Weekly*, offered me valuable advice. Denni Shefrin took a number of the photographs. Nancy Hammer has been a constant source of support. Neal Peirce has served as a mentor for many years; his engaging way of explaining complex subjects has always been an inspiration. Finally, I dedicate this book to William H. (Holly) Whyte who first taught me—27 years ago—to be a keen observer of city life. As this book was going to press in January 1999, Holly passed away at the age of 81. He will be missed.

Mark L. Hinshaw
January 1999

Seattle Citistate area

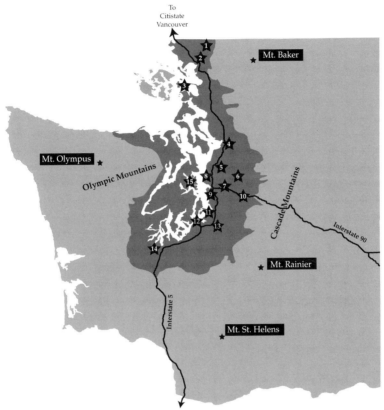

To
Citistate
Vancouver

★ Mt. Baker

Mt. Olympus ★

Olympic Mountains

Cascade Mountains

Interstate 90

Mt. Rainier

Interstate 5

To
Citistate
Portland

Mt. St. Helens ★

LEGEND	
Anacortes	3
Bainbridge Island	15
Bellevue	7
Bellingham	2
Everett	4
Federal Way	11
Issaquah	10
Kirkland	5
Lynden	1
Olympia	14
Puyallup	13
Redmond	6
Seattle	8
Tacoma	12
Tukwila	9

A Thumbnail Sketch of Seattle:
Geography, History, Economy (Sort Of)

In comparison with earlier city-states, like Athens or Florence, Seattle is more of an economic and cultural entity than a political one. Rather than extending its reach by sending out legions of soldiers, its expansionary techniques are more subtle and, perhaps, more insidious. Nordstrom opens encampments in other cities with great fanfare, showing its conquests not armaments but assurances that they will accept returned merchandise. Microsoft has managed, in less than two decades, to alter how virtually everyone in the world works and writes. Purveyors of espresso offer their addictive liquids in all manner of places, from world capitals like Tokyo and London to backroad hamlets like Gallatin, Montana. It may be mere coincidence, but many of the logos of Seattle coffee companies resemble the decorated disks held aloft on staffs by Roman armies.

From a political perspective, Citistate Seattle is a mess. The Puget Sound Basin, which defines the geographic limits, holds over 100 separate governmental units, not counting dozens of water and school districts. They rarely see eye to eye. Communities outside Seattle proper view it with suspicion. Adjacent communities squabble with one another over territory, taxes, and traffic impacts. Small town folk resent the liberal, elitist attitudes they see exhibited by inner city people, while urban dwellers scoff at what they see as suburban dullness.

That Citistate Seattle is so powerful, then, is nothing short of amazing. The numbers tell only part of the story. Almost 3.5 million people live within 7,000 square miles of land surrounding Puget Sound and lying between the Cascade Mountain range on the east and Olympic Mountain range on the west. The number of people is comparable to the populations of South Carolina and

1

Connecticut and only somewhat smaller than Colorado. These other places, in fact, make interesting comparisons. Like the charming southern state, Citistate Seattle is still small enough to exhibit a generous amount of small-town folksiness. Like the northeastern state, it is filled with folks who have relatively high incomes and a preference for proximity to urban amenities. And, like the Rocky Mountain state, it is packed with people who appreciate being surrounded by rugged terrain and untamed wilderness.

If it were a state of the union, it would be the 26th largest. Neither a behemoth bursting at the seams like California, nor a pastoral paradise like Wyoming. Which is not to say that it has no resemblance to either. Living in Citistate Seattle is like living with a gorgeous model who has a bi-polar disorder. The physical qualities may be breathtaking. But the periods of rambunctious frenzy alternating with months-long gloominess can be maddening. Not unlike quickly downing a double tall latte.

Over the past decade, Citistate Seattle has found itself the focus of considerable media attention. Films and television programs are regularly set here—both in urban and rural areas. *Sleepless in Seattle* accurately portrayed the loopy romance of the place. David Lynch's "Twin Peaks" best captured the combination of murkiness and mania. *Fortune* magazine has praised the investment potentials. *Money* magazine has gushed over the livability. But this is a relatively new phenomenon. As recently as the early 1980s, Seattle was a quiet, backwater province, with a boring skyline, a smattering of lackluster museums, and restaurants hardly worth writing about.

For most of its history, the economy of the region was inextricably linked with industries of resource extraction: fishing and the growing, harvesting and production of wood. With the decline of the timber industry, it has been years since one could be passed on the highway by huge logging trucks with their forked trailers piled high with 5-foot diameter logs. A combination of court decisions limiting fishing and the decline in the number of fish has produced a fishing fleet that is a mere remnant of its former self.

What propelled Seattle into the global economy was the Boeing Airplane Company, with its vast factories producing thousands of fighters and bombers during World War II. One of the most fascinating photographs of that era shows a huge Boeing plant enshrouded in a clever camouflage. On its multiacre roof was built a sprawling suburban subdivision, an eerie presage of those that followed the war. Four-foot-high houses and trees, together with yards and swimming pools, provided just enough topographic relief to fool the much-feared Japanese reconnaissance planes. Forever after, the regional economy was inextricably linked to the fate and fortune of the airline industry.

But possibly the best thing that happened to Seattle was the Boeing "bust" in 1969, when tens of thousands of workers were laid off, plunging the region into a deep recession for almost five years. If the region were to survive it had to nurture a wider range of businesses and adopt an ethic that balanced economic vitality with environmental values. It set out to do so and planted the seeds that later blossomed into a myriad of software and biotechnology companies. Several remarkable public actions created the foundation that continues to support and nurture contemporary Seattle.

Ten years prior to the Boeing downturn, county voters had passed a ballot measure creating Metro, a regional authority charged with intercepting and treating the raw sewage that for many decades had poured directly into Elliott Bay, Lake Union, and Lake Washington. By the 1970s, these signature water bodies were cleaned up and reinvigorated as visual and recreational amenities, as well as habitat for fish and wildlife. Metro also was given the task of operating a regional bus system, which it has steadily developed and expanded in the years since.

Another ballot measure passed in 1968 was called "Forward Thrust." It authorized $334 million to build parks, trails, community centers, sports facilities, and swimming pools throughout King County, leaving a legacy of solid, livable neighborhoods.

A subsequent bond issue allowed the county to purchase the "development rights" of hundreds of acres of remaining farmland before they were sold off and subdivided. Consequently, the urbanized area is occasionally interrupted by great swaths of verdant, open fields punctuated by barns and silos. And the Skagit Valley, a rich agricultural area occupying the northern reaches of the region, continues to support farming. In less than one hour, you can go from a desk on the 50th floor of an office tower to a stroll through seemingly endless ribbons of tulip fields.

The national economic boom of the 1980s helped push Citistate Seattle into prominence. The dramatic skyline, so photogenic from across the bay, graced front pages and magazine spreads. Microsoft changed virtually every aspect of how the country, and the world, worked. At least a dozen urban neighborhoods began to thrive, all separated from the destinations of tourists and all vibrant places for local folks to shop, eat, meet friends, see a movie, and just hang out. In recent years, Citistate Seattle has set to building, at the same time, sports stadiums and symphony halls, art museums and performing arts theaters. Voters have passed bond issues (read tax increases) to build rail transit, low-income housing, and schools at the same time that California and Oregon voters did exactly the opposite.

While it has been evolving, Citistate Seattle has acquired something of a mystique, a set of myths and legends generated by writers, visitors, and residents themselves. Some of these reflect reality, others are amusing in their sound-bite simplicity. Here are a handful, together with the "truth."

1. It rains all the time

It depends upon what you view as rain. In quantity, the amount of rain rarely exceeds 40 inches a year—about the same as New York City. But the amount is meted out in torturously small doses. We have much more of it in the fall and winter than in the spring and summer. But if Citistate Seattle had its own language, we would need to have a couple of dozen words for rain, similar to Eskimo terms for snow. Since we don't, here is a partial list of the many forms of moisture and precipitation we are subjected to:

Light rain
Moderate rain
Heavy rain
Showers with periods of sun (a favorite term of weather announcers)
Rainstorms
Cold rain
Spurts of rain
Bursts of rain
Teasing rain (start, stop, start, stop)
Spitting rain
Blowing rain
Horizontal rain
Upward blowing rain
Mist
Fog
Clouds (actually a more frequent characteristic than falling rain)
and
A general, pervasive dampness

Citistate Seattle is a water culture. Water shapes the landscape, determines the vegetation, and drives our power plants. We live on it and in it. Perhaps it is the reason why we are addicted to coffee. Since we cannot get enough warmth from the sun, we have devised a way to get it from the water.

2. Coffee is sold on every street corner

Sounds like an exaggeration, but it is really an understatement. Throughout the region, it is highly likely that espresso drinks can be bought in the following places:

Sidewalk espresso carts
Coffee bars
Cafes and restaurants

Bookstores
Magazine stores
McDonald's
Department stores
Hardware stores
Clinics
Hospitals
Gas stations
Movie theaters
Performing art theaters
7-Elevens
Ferries
Bus stations
Train stations
Airports
Museums
Motels
Hotels
Video stores
Zoos

Ironically, given that coffee is so clearly the local drug of choice, about the only place it is not sold is in drugstores.

3. Seattle is a company town

It is not a company town; it is a five company town. Or, at least it seems to be. The companies are Boeing, Microsoft, Nordstrom, Starbucks, and REI.

You can't drive anywhere without eventually passing a gargantuan Boeing plant. Boeing still is the economically stabilizing mainstay of the region. With recent mergers, its influence on global transportation almost constitutes a monopoly.

Nordstrom clothes us. Tales of the good will and extra effort by Nordstrom sales people have made for much dinner table conversation. Its new flagship store is the crown jewel in a merchandising empire that has swept across the country and scared the pants off the competitors.

Each workday begins by looking at the Microsoft logo on our computer screens. The sprawling, Xanadu-like home of the richest-man-of-the-world Bill Gates on the eastern shore of Lake Washington is now a major attraction for tour boat operators.

Starbucks is another phenomenon. People who have lived here more than 20 years still recall the original shop long before the modest business was purchased by entrepreneur Howard Schultz. Starbucks is now a national icon and a bellwether of reinvestment in numerous neighborhoods. Generally unknown to outsiders, though, are at least a dozen other coffee vendors offering equal or superior blends.

REI (Recreational Equipment Inc.), for some, is a lifestyle itself. Its huge, architecturally aggressive store, perched on the edge of Interstate 5, is almost always packed with true believers fingering and discussing the latest in recreational gear and freeze-dried comestibles. It is cooperatively owned by card-carrying consumer/members. Having a low membership number (meaning longstanding) is definitely a symbol of status.

4. Everyone wears flannel shirts, down jackets, and work boots
False.

I think people are confusing us with Oregon. And I'm not just kidding. Not too many years ago, *Time* magazine ran a story that referred to Seattle, Oregon. I have not worn flannel for years. And, while I own several suits, I also have a pair of work boots. The boots are made from recycled milk bottles and the sole is stamped with the words: "Reduce Reuse Recycle."

5. Californians are universally despised
True.

Unless you have a friend who is from California. Or a relative. Or you are. Which is very often the case.

So Citistate Seattle is defined by software and sportswear, topography and water—all making for a unique combination of high technology and high adventure. Its aircraft connect us to the global economy. And its coffee both soothes us and makes us crazy.

I

City Centers

Denni Shefrin

In the early 1990s, the legislature of the State of Washington did a remarkable and surprising thing. Though long dominated by a conservative majority drawn largely from smaller, rural towns and counties, it passed a strong, far-reaching act intended to manage and direct growth. Not that this was done willingly. After 10 years of rapid development within and around Seattle—fueled by land speculation, available capital, federal tax breaks, and an influx of folks from California and other parts of the country—the citizenry had had enough.

A coalition of neighborhood activists and environmentalists crafted a ballot initiative designed to curb sprawl, property tax increases, traffic jams, and despoiled wilderness. Although completely draconian in its attempts at clamping down on development, it appealed to angry voters and seemed on the verge of passing.

Hoping to dissuade their constituents, both the governor and the legislature pledged to pass a more reasonable, but effective, law if the initiative were voted down. It was. So the Growth Management Act was born. Actually, two laws were passed; one in 1990 and another in 1991. The statutes swept into place a series of striking provisions. Some of these, such as the Urban Growth Boundary concept, were borrowed from Oregon. The idea of concurrency—that development would be linked to infrastructure improvements—was taken from Florida. But given the strong tradition of local control throughout the state, there was to be no top-down, heavy-handed state bureaucracy to control it all. In fact, once local councils adopted their plans, the plans would be presumed to be in compliance with state law.

Nevertheless, the GMA rocked local governments to their foundations. They had to declare environmentally sensitive lands off-limits to development. They were forced to talk to one another and mutually agree upon future population targets and growth limits. They had to pass policies that addressed numerous criteria, including land use, transportation, community facilities, and housing affordability. Squirm though they did, no city or county got off the hook. (Actually, the law did not require those counties with low rates of growth to prepare plans.)

A regional plan called "Vision 2020" was put forward. Shepherded by the Puget Sound Regional Council—a coalition of local governmental bodies—the document constituted an agreement about how and where to grow. Several previous efforts had failed to galvanize local leaders, but this time all the pieces fell into place. All counties and cities, as well as the state, would take a consistent and coordinated approach to land-use decisions and transportation investments, focusing development into existing cities. One of the most remarkable results of this collective planning was the designation of a dozen "urban centers" throughout the region into which *more and denser* development would be channeled, in return for no longer expanding outward.

Policies had to be followed by revised regulations within two years. And communities were obligated to build things: streets, sidewalks, parks, schools, trails, utilities, etc. Transit would also play a role in community development. A few years later, voters in Puget Sound passed a multi-county bond issue to set up a regional transit authority to provide commuter trains, light rail trains, and an expanded bus service.

As one might suspect, the real estate industry bolted. The GMA was roundly attacked as frustrating consumers' desires for large houses, estate living, and low density. The industry helped finance a "Property Rights" initiative, the clear purpose of which was to gut growth management. Fortunately, the ballot measure was soundly defeated. Still protesting, the building folks continue to moan. Who in the Pacific Northwest would want to live downtown? Who would want to live in row houses? Who would want to live above shops? Who would ride transit instead of four-wheel drives?

The jury may still be out on the last question, but the verdict is definitely in on the former. Downtowns throughout the region are thriving, bustling with shops, theaters, and—yes—dense urban housing. All sorts of new housing forms are now being built and people cannot get enough of them. The robust regional economy of the late 1990s was now enriched by choices previously all but unknown.

The chapters in this section describe a number of places that offer the new choices available in Citistate Seattle. Not all of it is wonderful. Not all of it is universally welcome. The results are clearly mixed. But with each new experiment, each new step, the path is blazed to the next one. We are finally coming to terms with what it means to live in an urban region.

1

Pike Place Market: The Soul of Seattle

The Pike Place Public Market is a truly amazing place. Approximately four blocks long and two blocks wide, it is perched on a bluff facing Elliott Bay. Roughly resembling an Italian hill town, it is an assemblage of numerous, oddly shaped structures. Buildings on pilings. Flatiron buildings. Stepped buildings with multiple basements. Old buildings. New buildings. Renovated buildings.

The market is filled with fishmongers, vegetable sellers, butchers, and fruit vendors. Craftspeople jostle for tables brimming with assorted, hand-made goods. Some of it is inside, some of it is outside. There are full-service, high-priced restaurants and cheap, cozy cafes. Shops carry used clothing, books, antiques, kitchenware, wine, fresh bread, pastries, plants, herbs, tea and coffee, jewelry, glass art, comic books, and assorted tchotchkes. If one is in the mood for shopping, a trip to the market can yield a one-of-a-kind silver ring or an out-of-print book on Marxist dialectics. If one is peckish, the market offers everything from paper-wrapped piroshkies to a well-presented platter of Penn Cove mussels.

The market is a microcosm of the Citistate Seattle. It offers abundant opportunities for small scale, entrepreneurial creativity to thrive. Personalized, friendly, face-to-face communication is proffered instead of packaged products and experiences. Like real life, these transactions can be a bit unpredictable and risky; you need to be somewhat street wise and knowledgeable to get a good bargain. The market demands that you explore it and engage it. It is not a mere "tourist attraction" or one of the many ersatz "festival markets" that have been so popular in recent years.

The intersection of Pike Street with Pike Place forms "ground zero" of the Pike Place Market.

Parts of the place are smelly and nasty. Like a Middle Eastern bazaar or an Asian shopping street, the air is filled with strange and wonderful sights, sounds, and smells. People jostle one another, yell out, sing, play music, hawk their wares, and noisily converse over a meal or a drink. Anyone foolish enough to try to drive along Pike Place immediately discovers the mistake. Cars move slower than people on foot. Pedestrians have the power to criss-cross wherever and whenever they wish. The market demonstrates the tension and behavior of people competing for the use of limited space—just as we are now doing throughout the region.

The Market also demonstrates our fondness for messy democracy. The place is governed by a myriad of organizations. The Pike Place Market Preservation and Development Authority—an independent arm of the city—owns and manages the real estate. The Pike Place Merchants Association is the advocate for sellers of goods and services, and the Market Constituency represents craftspeople. The Pike Place Historical Commission protects the place from intrusion by chains, franchises, and inappropriate architecture. Battles of differing perspectives occasionally break out; alliances are forged, petitions are passed around. In the end, the Market emerges reinvigorated.

The Market was saved from near destruction by a citizens initiative in 1971. The city and the downtown business community had intended for most of it to be demolished and replaced by towering condominiums, offices, and parking structures. A small fragment of the original would have been retained as a quaint artifact. But, the initiative called for something else. A market district would be established. A core area of older buildings would be completely

Above: Pike Place Market is a compact, walkable district of shops, cafes, vendors, luxury housing, and low-income housing. Left: Local vendors jostle with tourists amid the colorful array of vegetable, fruit, and fish vendors.

restored. New buildings, including shops and housing could go up around the perimeter, outside the historic center. And a permanent agency would shepherd its renovation under the close scrutiny of a citizen board. The initiative passed by a healthy margin.

It took almost 20 years for the market to completely re-do itself. (One parcel still remains untouched.) But the result is absolutely splendid. Some of the restored buildings were so faithfully done that the only visible difference between the before and after condition is the absence of grime on the walls.

In the late 1970s, another initiative was placed on the ballot for King County voters to decide. The question was whether to tax ourselves to come up with $50 million to purchase remaining farmlands in the county. The campaign was brilliant. Mailers, posters, radio spots, and roadside signs linked the potential loss of agricultural land with the possibility that Pike Place Market would also disappear. The bond issue passed overwhelmingly.

Clearly, the Pike Place Market is a place that many, many people feel strongly about. It is a symbol that we care about our history, our environment, and our culture. It stands for the things we value most highly. It appeals both to conservative capitalists who champion individual rights and to liberals who rally around collective responsibilities.

Citistate Seattle is a place that tries to balance both ideals: the value of the individual and the value of community. The Market is a constant, living reminder to ourselves that it can be done.

2

Getting It Right in the Regrade

For several years in the early 1980s, I lived in the Denny Regrade, a neighborhood at the north end of downtown Seattle. The apartment was in a solid but plain brick building from the 1920s. It was one of a number that were constructed immediately after a massive public works project flattened Denny Hill. For almost a decade, the huge hill was shoveled and sluiced into Elliott Bay.

My apartment building was hardly charming, but it did have a certain dignity that spoke of an in-town neighborhood. People lived in the place not for the views but for the convenience to the cornucopia of downtown.

The building, as well as the neighborhood, seemed to appeal to people who were bit quirky. Dolores, my next door neighbor, kept her apartment filled with waist-high stacks of magazines, books, boxes, clothes, and miscellaneous bric-a-brac, with only a two-foot-wide pathway snaking through it all. When I lived there during the early 1980s, the city seemed not to consider the area a true neighborhood. Street crews would frequently tear up the streets all night long, just yards from people's windows. Meter checkers were fond of leaping out precisely at 8 a.m. on Saturdays, leaving a wake of tickets on residents' cars.

In the early '90s, the Regrade began to take off, with restaurants, shops, art galleries, nightspots, and thousands of new apartments and condominiums. Numerous buildings were renovated, and new buildings went up, seemingly, on every other block. Much of the new stuff was unremarkable; some of it was downright terrible. In particular, the blocky apartment buildings along Elliott Avenue, with the relentlessly repetitive, pulpit-sized balconies added little in the way of character to a corridor that badly needs some.

A few projects were commendable in their efforts to give something back to the neighborhood. The Alexandria showed how to disguise an otherwise boring parking garage with a bit of whimsy, using human figures cut out of metal. Over at Lenora Street and Terry Avenue, there is a delightful combination of renovation and new construction in an apartment complex for low-income people—evidence that good design can be accomplished even where the budget is tight. Too bad that its neighbor to the south is so dreadful, with its jumble of units stacked atop a huge, flat wall painted a bizarre shade of red and decorated with flimsy metal trellises.

The best new development in the Denny Regrade, though, has to be Belltown Court. This is the first project that doesn't offer just housing, but helps build the neighborhood.

Belltown Court doesn't just offer housing, it helps build the Denny Regrade neighborhood.

Belltown Court recognizes its surroundings. Its brick-faced ground floor sits squarely on the edge of the sidewalk, with no setbacks or barren plazas. What lines the street is exactly what should line the street in an urban neighborhood: shops and cafes. There is a fine, neighborhood-style pizza place, a terrific baker, an elegant Italian bistro, and several other spots serving up ethnic food. At the corner of First and Wall is a little grocery store and delicatessen—exactly what is needed to serve local residents.

So much of the retail space that has been built around the city these days has been too big, badly designed, or poorly located. Consequently it has remained vacant. Here, care was taken to make sure that tenant spaces were sufficiently small in order to attract small enterprises. And the designers created shop fronts that look like shop fronts, not office space. Painted wood trim around doors and window, display windows with sills a foot or two above the sidewalk, and spaces with appropriately high ceilings convey the traditional feeling of streetside shops. These few "rules" may be obvious and simple, but they seem to be done hardly ever these days.

Belltown Court comprises two separate buildings, separated by an alley that provides access to parking and deliveries. A portion of the alley is spanned by a deck that connects the two structures and provides a sizable chunk of outdoor space. An exercise room, a glass-enclosed lap pool, and a common recreation room face this landscaped interior courtyard, as do many of the units. The "view" is quite restful and soothing; it shows that downtown housing need not depend upon views to be marketable.

The interior spaces of Belltown Court set a new standard for apartments in this city. The elegant entrance lobbies have high ceilings, deco-style lighting, fine furnishings, and artwork. The corridors feel homey, not like the narrow institutional hallways usually found in most apartment buildings. The apartments themselves have generous amounts of glass, interesting spaces, and fine woodwork.

One of the surprising things about Belltown Court is that some residents have young children. Contrary to popular mythology, families can live just fine in a downtown. However, since the developer did not expect this type of household, no play space was provided for children. It might have been possible for some portion of the roof to be converted to such a use, but, alas, there is no elevator access.

It is Belltown Court's facades on First Avenue and Second Avenue that exhibit an exceptional understanding of how to create an urban neighborhood. Each facade is different, reflecting varied conditions on the two streets. The First Avenue side is flat-topped, reflecting a number of older structures that are nearby.

On the Second Avenue facade, brickwork on the first floor incorporates horizontal banding, echoing the banding used on the older apartment building across the street. It is so rare to find buildings that make courteous gestures to already existing buildings.

The upper portion of the Second Avenue side includes a number of clever elements. The balconies, though on the small side, seem more generous with their finely scaled, open metalwork. The bays and terraces are not identical; there are several variations. A bold, slanted roof form—punctuated by peaked dormers—graces the top of the building. The effect is similar to a block of row houses, which are identical at first glance, but actually contain subtle differences.

Belltown Court suggests that we finally know how to create denser forms of housing that are not just merely "units" stacked and packed into minimalist containers. The development provides a real sense of home for the people who live there and contributes richness and variety to the neighborhood around it.

To some people, Belltown Court may seem a bit eccentric in its design and color palette. But like my idiosyncratic former neighbor Delores, it fits the neighborhood perfectly.

3

Culture and Commerce

Downtown Minneapolis in the late 1950s offered an astonishing array of cultural choices for a pre-teenager. For the cost of a bus ticket into town, it was possible to walk to a wide range of cultural attractions.

The main library was expansive and comfortable. Next door, the planetarium was cool, dark, and mysterious. The Institute of Art exhibited classic works of art, while the Walker Art Center excelled in showing modern pieces. The Walker's hands-on programs for children left a lasting influence on many young people living in that city—including me.

The public school system encouraged appreciation for the arts by regularly busing kids to see rehearsals of the symphony and theatrical productions. Even now, I can still feel myself sitting in a lushly appointed hall, with enormous chandeliers, sconces, and decorative carvings, fingering a shiny program while enveloped in velvet upholstery. Just passing through the vast lobby, with its cavernous upper mezzanine, quickened the pulse.

Only a few of the many contemporary theaters that I have been in since then have engendered that kind of visceral response. Over the last 30 years we have built a spate of Spartan theaters throughout the country. Perhaps budgets were lean. Maybe modern architects could not countenance any form of embellishment. Or possibly the people who championed these spare spaces thought that the architecture might get in the way of the performance.

Whatever the reasons, what was forgotten was that attending a live production of theater or music involves a whole host of auditory, visual, and tactile impressions, infusing the experience with emotional impact. Many contemporary theaters reflect the supermarket school of architecture—paste a fancy facade onto the front of a big, boring box.

A few years ago, these impoverished ideas of designing performance spaces began to change. For a while, movie theaters were actually being designed

Courtesy of Callison Architects

The former Eagles Fraternal Lodge was converted into a mixed use development combining theater spaces and low-income housing on the upper floors. Callison Architects designed the theaters. GGLO designed the housing.

with more elegance and elan than live theaters. Great glass lobbies, with sparkling lights and even art, began to reappear. Both the exteriors and the interiors of the buildings suggested the drama, comedy, and mystery that awaited inside.

The design of buildings for live theater and music seemed to have been stuck in the notion that high culture must be enjoyed in monastic surroundings. Flat, unadorned walls, save for the obligatory piece or two of public art. Enough lineal feet of pipe railing to outfit a federal penitentiary. Lobbies designed with less flair than you might find in the waiting room of a bus station.

The restoration of the Fifth Avenue Theatre in downtown Seattle in the early '80s reminded us of the places we had begun to lose. More recently, the splendid renovation of the Paramount Theatre added a new dimension of drama to downtown. The new ACT (A Contemporary Theatre) theater, housed in the structure built back in 1925 for the Fraternal Order of Eagles, is the result of an almost miraculous makeover.

What a complex and complicated project! As a producer of live theatrical productions, ACT moved its principal venue from its existing location on lower Queen Anne and dramatically expanded its operations by creating two

One of the new theater spaces was fitted into the former ballroom of the old lodge hall.

additional performance spaces. Each of these spaces came with difficult design issues involving "back of the house" support, access, emergency exiting, lighting, loading.

Because the building was historic and contained legally protected interior spaces, federal, state, and local approvals were necessary. This was hardly an easy task since the space needs for the theater unavoidably required demolition of the Eagles lodge hall.

Halfway through the design process, ACT decided to bring all of its functions, including the scenery shops, together within the Eagles building. This required adding two new floors onto the roof and getting approvals all over again from regulatory agencies. Construction of the lower theater necessitated excavation below the water table.

Funding the theater, which exceeded $30 million, required major financial commitments from corporations, foundations, and individuals, with some critical donations coming in only at the eleventh hour.

If all this weren't enough, the project was made even more complex by including 44 units of affordable housing in renovated rooms on the upper floors.

With the exterior of the Eagles Building meticulously restored, the terra cotta sparkles with new life. Inside, the place is not unlike discovering a series of secret compartments, each revealing a new set of architectural delights.

The building is a wonderfully mysterious maze of vestibules and lobbies, anterooms, theater spaces, a curious cabaret with cryptic symbols on the ceiling, an elegant formal reception hall, lounges, stairs, offices, rehearsal rooms, shops, and numerous other spaces that support the performances.

There are two sloped-floor theaters, one stacked on top of the other. The lower one is a traditional deign with a thrust stage and the upper one is a more unconventional configuration with an asymmetrically shaped arena. The latter, inserted into the grand old, Beaux Arts-styled ballroom, looks like an alien spacecraft that somehow managed to find a docking station inside the building. The effect is breathtaking.

The importance of the new ACT Theatre goes well beyond the benefits of having another cultural venue. Together with the Paramount, the Fifth Avenue, the Cineplex Odeon complex, Pacific Place, the nearby Nordstrom, and the planned convention center expansion, ACT will contribute to the complete transformation of this previously disjointed part of downtown Seattle.

Indeed, this district promises to emerge as a new center of nightlife, with blazing marquees, bright lights, opening night galas, classy cafes and cabarets, and places for civic celebrations. A place, perhaps, not unlike Picadilly Circus in London, the Stroget in Copenhagen, or the Theatre District in Toronto.

The ACT Theatre blends the new with the old and anchors a part of downtown that was, until now, a cultural backwater. It brings new life both to the stage and the streets around it.

4

Dining Downtown

Dozens of Seattle's 400 downtown restaurants offer sidewalk seating in good weather.

Pick any side street in midtown Manhattan and you will find a least one small, "secret" restaurant that manages to be both animated and intimate. Usually the bar is right in the middle and the kitchen is in plain sight. Often the decor is simple and understated, but sometimes there is an extravaganza of forms, colors, and details.

These "cool" cafes are never part of a corporate empire, with contrived themes and menus. Rather, they are individually owned, with the proprietor positioned right near the door to greet patrons, not unlike the act of gracious-

Bryce Thomas, architect with Millet Associates, transformed this previously non-descript storefront into a quirky night spot.

ly receiving guests into a home. The effect is warm and welcoming; you get an immediate feeling that you are about to be taken care of.

Until the past decade, Seattle did not have many of these kinds of places. Sure, wait staff could be personable and perky (sometimes too perky) and the food could be fine. But there is nothing like seeing a real live person reflected in all aspects of the place from the selections to the service to the surroundings. The soul of a place can be clearly felt only when the owner is obviously present.

In recent years, we have picked up a bunch of these little gems. Though a number are scattered about the city, there is a concentration of them in the Denny Regrade. First Avenue, in particular, is filled with them. It's hard to find a block without at least one terrific "boite."

Several of these new restaurants display interiors that are the loving reflection of their owner's tastes in decor. Lampreia, one of the first to appear, was carved out of a low-ceilinged corner of Belltown Court apartments. Owner/chef Scott Carsberg used a few simple touches to create an elegant, serene, understated atmosphere. The slightly recessed entry trimmed with wood and displaying a menu is a sophisticated touch.

A few doors to the south, the Belltown Pub displays high-backed booths of fine craftsmanship. Like a true pub—though an uncharacteristic non-smoking one—the place is splendidly convivial. People can easily run into and chat with

The inside of this cafe and nightclub in the Belltown neighborhood is a contrast of old and new.

old acquaintances.

Around the corner on Second, Shiro's is a tiny, but supremely well crafted, place that serves Japanese cuisine that is artful in both taste and presentation. The interior includes fine woodwork and inlaid flooring patterns, and the display cases in the vestibule are filled with delicate Asian artifacts.

Over on Third Avenue, cater-corner from the Bon Marche, lies a hideaway called Isabella. The drawn curtains may give the impression that the place is closed, but be assured that inside it is lively and urbane. As with many of these recent places, the bar is closely connected with the dining room, adding a lively energy. Owner Gino Borriello splashed the walls with several slightly primary colors, a scheme that doesn't sound like it would work but does. Like his compatriots, Gino is affable and gracious, offering a genuine smile and good-natured conversation that no chain restaurant can hope to provide. Isabella serves up exquisite fare within surroundings of quiet repose. Here the people are on display, at least as much as the decor.

At the opposite end of the spectrum, Marco's Supper Club is intense, animated, and frenetic. The clutch of closely packed tables placed hard up against the bar makes it feel like one of the beautiful and boisterous places around Union Square in San Francisco. The atmosphere is so thick that it is possible to engage in absolutely shameless behavior and barely be noticed.

Marco's owner Marco Rulff explains that the "bar" is not legally a bar but rather is classified as a "lunch counter." Hence, no separation from the dining area is necessary. During the summer months the rear courtyard is charming but somewhat overwhelmed by the tall, generic residential towers that surround it.

Some restaurants are spectacular settings for socializing and supping. The Flying Fish is a landmark along First Avenue. During the summer, even on a rainy, blustery evening, the place is inviting and engaging. Its great, glass roll-up windows open the place to the street.

Restaurateur Paul McKay recently opened two new restaurants in the area—one stacked atop the other. El Gaucho is above the Pampas Room. Entering each with its flamboyant decor feels like one has just walked onto the stage of a Broadway musical.

One place goes only by its address: "2218" is a grand combination of spaces, forms, material, and lighting. Two meticulously detailed staircases ascend to small, secretive spaces above the main floor. The row of columns that formerly held up the roof were removed and replaced with enormous beams from which hangs an angular-shaped mezzanine. A dramatically lighted brick wall at the rear lends an element of intrigue.

The bar is ideal for a late afternoon liaison. At night, the place jumps with music. The presence of live musicians on weeknights make 2218 feel like an intimate nightclub, though one that is slightly sinister. The long vertical crack in the sidewall of plaster seems to be straight from Roman Polanski's demented film *Repulsion.*

So why have these splendid little, one-of-a-kind places suddenly appeared on the local scene? Several explanations are possible.

The old style of hell-raising bars where guys would knock back beers and hassle female patrons are definitely, and thankfully, socially passe. So are smoke-filled lounges filled with emaciated alcoholics. People want to simply enjoy good food and conversation in pleasant and sociable surroundings. So these restaurants may be simply responding to current social trends.

Another plausible reason is our growing interest in fine, regional cuisine. "Theme" restaurants with their ostentatious decor and contrived menus are no match for good, personalized places. Many of these new restaurants place their kitchens in visually prominent locations to assure us that we are getting the real goods under the watchful eye of the owner.

Furthermore, we are finally seeing the density of downtown living that Seattle has long been seeking. Urban dwellers want local spots that offer variety, value, and verve.

Whatever the reason, we are fortunate to finally have a whole new set of choices concentrated in a relatively small part of town that is eminently walkable, endlessly fascinating, and getting better all the time.

5

Why Aren't There Any Great Buildings in Belltown?

The best piece of architecture in Belltown isn't a building at all. It's a garden. A P-patch. The Belltown P-patch to be specific.

Its metal gate laced with gnarled garden tools is absolutely charming. The decorative fencing is beautiful. And the *pique assiette* tilework is both mysterious and exquisite.

The Banner Building has scooped up a pile of design awards, which are certainly well-deserved. And Belltown Court is a splendid prototype for urban/mixed use/infill housing. But, even so, Belltown has almost no buildings—old or new—that would cause me to weep if they suddenly were to disappear.

Except for that precious little garden.

The P-patch reminds me of Belltown the way it was a few years back—before it got to be one of the trendiest neighborhoods in the region. To be sure, Belltown is becoming an interesting place to live, to dine on some of the best food the city has to offer, and to just hang out. It's relatively safe. It's relatively attractive. And it's relatively lively. A downtown neighborhood that most cities would kill to have.

So what is missing? Strolling around the P-patch as I did in mid-June on a warm weekday morning immediately brought to mind what the Regrade in general and Belltown in particular may have lost. The P-patch is funky. It is weird. It is laid back. And it shows the sign of many hands and minds, creatively and quirkily pushing things around, throwing things up, and changing it all from time to time. The P-patch represents a naive fearlessness that helps make a place not just good but great.

Belltown is packed with shops and sidewalk cafes that are lively well into the evening hours.

The Flying Fish is a fine restaurant, with a great visual style. But, when I look at that corner, I still see the dozen or so brightly painted doors that Ann Gardner, Carl Smool, and their friends nailed up after a drunk crashed into the building 10 years ago.

And, though First Avenue is almost awash with cool boites and boutiques, I sorely miss Ben Marks's way-before-its-time Belltown Cafe. That adventurous little diner, with its working-class counter, display of cryptic, hand-colored post cards, and restrooms reached off a ramshackle rear porch was, to me at least, indicative of a goofy energy and spirit that seems to have diminished.

Architecturally, Seattle is a very reticent city. Almost as if people are afraid to make a social blunder that might offend someone. Perhaps it is our Scandinavian heritage that sets us up for tidiness and order. Or, perhaps, we've been working so hard at becoming a cosmopolitan/commercial/cultural hub of the

Pacific Rim that we've taken ourselves way too seriously. Maybe all that turgid praise in magazines like *Newsweek* and *Fortune* has given us a collective complex.

Despite the amazing talent we have in the design community, we can't seem to get a building that truly sings in the very place that we should expect to find one. Belltown has many of the trappings, but little of the true texture, of a great urban place.

It could be argued that Belltown needs no great buildings. Belltown is more a sociological phenomenon than an architectural one. It is beginning to build up layers of wonderful stuff. Stylish shops like Paragon. Little cafes like Macrina. Fringe theater spaces like The Annex. The Speakeasy. The Crocodile. The Lux. Lush Life. The list keeps getting longer.

And then there is all the new housing, much of it aimed at people with modest incomes. Older, early Regrade apartment buildings sit amongst a spate of glitzy new condominiums. The mix of stuff is getting better and richer. Belltown now even has a direct connection to the waterfront. The Bell Street bridge at the north end of the Art Institute leads to the spectacular rooftop terrace at Pier 66.

But there are some disturbing trends as well. It should be clear enough that much of that new development is simply too big to frame the streets with proportions and details that make other neighborhoods like Fremont so endlessly interesting. The designers of Belltown Court have shown that this can be done. Too bad more architects don't seem even to try.

The street improvements along Second are more insipid than inspired. The shiny metal light poles belong more to some suburban industrial park. The broken brackets straight out of Dogpatch are amusing, but why bother installing clocks so small that you can barely read them? The pretend planks strewn along the sidewalks are too simple-minded to be even mildly interesting.

So let me offer up three principles for Belltown—principles that might produce buildings and public spaces with more verve, as well as nerve.

With a slight apology to Daniel Burnham, the first principle is: "Make no big plans; such plans stultify the soul." Belltown, at its best, is made up of a myriad of small parts, each reflecting the decision of an individual property owner, merchant, artist, or whoever happens to be on the street.

Buildings that consume an entire block, no matter how well designed, violate this essential pattern. Belltown Court does a commendable job of producing an illusion, in part, of multiple buildings, But it's still a big box. Buildings in Belltown should be small—probably no larger that a quarter of a block—increments that differ with changes in technology and style.

The incredibly slender John Carney apartment building on First near Broad is a perfect example of this principle being applied to the ground. The building actually wraps around its neighbor to the south, but from the front is a diminutive, delightful addition to the street.

At Third and Bell, the Marvin Gardens fits the scale of Belltown. Even its units are small, lived in by folks who use the city as their living room. Too bad the sidewalk level is so miserably embellished. What might have been a great, gregarious building is merely clumsy.

The second principle is to lay out a whole bunch of welcome mats. This could be manifest in very big things, like, say: A little city hall, like those in other Seattle neighborhoods. A compact community center like the one on Vancouver's Granville Island. A small, storefront library. Or a school. These are all places that bring the community together in a set of shared experiences and interests. Buildings containing these functions could be vibrant statements of civic life, contemporary landmarks, celebratory symbols. But please, if one of these does come about, let's not allow the usual "community involvement" process to squeeze the life out of it.

Welcome mats can also be small. Certainly it helps to have places like Marco's, the Belltown Pub, and the Lux set out tables and chairs. But why isn't there one good newsstand—like you see in every urban neighborhood from L.A. to New York? And why are there no sidewalk vendors? Those wide sidewalks on Second should be used for something other than what looks for all the world to be a Christmas tree farm. And some real, wood benches with backs, please—the kind you might really want to sit on.

Finally, the last principle may be the most important one.

Belltown needs some maracas amid the symphony of soothing strings and melodious clarinets. Maracas invite you to join the party and dance. They make you feel a bit foolish. As instruments, they are rambunctious and, sometimes, even a bit annoying. But they get your attention.

Belltown needs a few really rambunctious buildings. Buildings that snap your neck back. Buildings that piss you off, they're so outrageous. Buildings that are hilarious. If we can't bring ourselves to do it, let's haul up some of the designers that turned West Hollywood's Melrose Avenue into some of the best architectural street theater anywhere.

The 2218 is almost there. But the coffee cup should have been twice the size. And giving off a trail of steam. Or it could have been tipped, sloshing its contents in frozen form just above the heads of pedestrians. Belltown could benefit from a large dose of urban street humor. Right now, it's just way too somber.

Except for the P-patch.

I hope that the Gothic, low-tech tendrils that hold aloft the high-tech solar panel in the garden will inspire someone to build a big architectonic duck right in the heart of Belltown. Enough already with those decorated sheds!

6

A Village Grows in Bellevue

Several years ago, Norm Rice, then the mayor of Seattle, introduced the idea of creating "urban villages." They were advanced as a way of accommodating additional new households, supporting public transit, and producing a concentration of amenities and services for residents. Looking for a catchy phrase to capture the idea of growth management, the mayor gave the term a fresh spin. It had initially been coined 30 years before by Columbia University sociologist Herbert Gans. Gans applied the phrase to the tightly knit weave of families, institutions, and businesses found in certain Boston neighborhoods.

Perhaps because it is unusual for a big city mayor to promote a city planning concept, the proposal attracted considerable attention, both nationally as well as locally. Throughout the Puget Sound region, communities of all sizes stared thinking about how to create urban villages. Though seemingly an oxymoron, the term evokes a gut level response in our collective American psyche. Many of us would prefer to live in a small town like the mythical Bedford Falls of *It's a Wonderful Life,* with its friendliness, folksiness, and sense of community. But few of us can actually do so, given that most jobs are found in metropolitan areas.

Many of the villages designated in the Seattle plan are places that have existed for quite a number of decades. Some, like Ballard, Madison Park, and Columbia City, used to be streetcar communities. These places, for the most part, already are urban villages.

A much more difficult challenge is how to create a sense of village in locations where there are few existing ingredients. What do we do when there is no "there" there?

Right now a new urban village is beginning to emerge in a place where, just a few years ago, there was hardly anything at all. On the edge of downtown Bellevue, along N.E. 12th Street, a number of things have been coming togeth-

The new regional library, designed by ZGF Architects, frames a public space that serves as a "village green" for this new urban neighborhood.

Timothy Hursley

er that can give us some ideas about how to establish villages in areas that were skipped over in the post-war rush to expand out into the countryside. It is also a place where several projects that are the work of some of the best design talent in the Northwest can be found.

The Ashwood district had been a typical suburban neighborhood of modest wood frame houses around an elementary school. As family sizes shrank, the school was eventually closed. Given the area's proximity to the downtown core, the city adopted a new set of regulations for it that encouraged higher density residential development to be done within a framework of design guidelines. For a number of years not much happened, but recently the area has begun to change dramatically.

Much of this change has been stimulated by some key public improvements. The centerpiece of the neighborhood is the new Bellevue Regional Library, built by the King County Library District. A spectacular building, it recalls the era of solid, monumental libraries that were constructed earlier in this century. Many of these still stand today as prominent and treasured landmarks, and

NBBJ Architects

NBBJ Architects designed this museum to evoke the qualities of a doll house.

Courtesy of Callison Architects

Park Place Condominiums is one of a half dozen major housing developments that have added over 1,000 dwelling units to this new urban neighborhood in downtown Bellevue.

this library promises to fill a similar role.

The library contains two grand interior spaces. One is a long, high galleria that separates the library itself from a row of public meeting rooms and allows them to be used independently of the hours of the library. There is a small used bookstore at one end that is operated by the Friends of the Library. The galleria is filled with art: bold paintings by Garth Edwards, an allegorical relief by Rich Beyer, and lights by Walter White. The library itself also contains a magnificent, multistory central space with a grand staircase leading to the three levels of stacks and reading rooms.

There are many delightful touches throughout the building. The area for children is a colorful collection of whimsical shapes and enclosures. Traditional, solid-looking oak armchairs are scatted throughout. The place is filled with nooks and crannies in which to squirrel away with a book.

The space in front of the building serves as an urban square. The design includes seating, water, and prominent artwork. The vacant, city-owned parcel next to the library has been reserved for a future public building and park. Bisecting the block will be a broad promenade, half of which has been built as a part of the library project.

To the northwest is a little building that is startling in its intricacy and exacting detail. The Rosalie Whyel Museum of Doll Art is an exquisite example of fine craftsmanship. The purpose of this privately funded museum seems to cause some degree of mirth among certain people, particularly of the male gender (while a museum containing model trains, of course, would not). Those who might think this subject to be frivolous would be mistaken. This is a superbly presented collection of miniatures that demonstrates customs, clothing, and manners through centuries of time. The museum also demonstrates the unexpected response that can be generated by the private sector to new directions set forth by public policy.

While the library and the museum were under construction, the city was building an entirely new street. The design team for N.E. 10th Street included not only engineers but architects and landscape architects. As a result, the sidewalks are generous in width and include benches, pedestrian-scaled lighting, and decorative paving.

A hallmark of an urban village is a variety of housing for different households and income levels. In recent years, the Ashwood area has seen the development of more than 1,000 dwelling units, from low rise apartments to high rise condominiums. The Pacific Regent complex is for senior citizens and offers "life care" facilities ranging from independent living to skilled nursing. A subsequent phase is planned for the space now occupied by a parking lot.

Along N.E. 12th Street is Park Place, a mid-rise condominium development. One of the most urbane multiple family projects on the Eastside, it is a finely scaled and well-detailed building with shops on the street level. The building is relatively dense (about 80 units per acre), but it doesn't look it. Its six stories are stair-stepped and capped by a cascading sloped roof.

A few hundred feet east of Park Place is Parkridge, a cluster of four apartment buildings built atop underground parking. As with Park Place, no land has been wasted on surface parking. The same developer is building several hundred additional apartments on a block to the south.

The emerging Ashwood neighborhood in Bellevue is certainly not yet a complete "urban village"; it is now more like a fragment of one. But it is a good start, considering that virtually nothing was there to build on. It could use some good neighborhood stores, and they will likely come as more people move in. The planned park is sorely needed but is waiting for funding from the city. But, so far, the place is shaping up as a good example of what cooperative efforts by government and the private sector can accomplish.

7

Revitalizing Everett

My first full-time job was in the city of Hoboken, New Jersey. Every day, I would take the train from midtown Manhattan to the town on the west side of the Hudson River. Virtually the only "reverse" commuter to Hoboken, I would leave the station and enter a city that seemed to be dying.

Back in the early '70s, Hoboken was a sad place. Its factories had closed or were closing. Its formerly bustling harborfront was silent, lined with abandoned pier sheds and warehouses. Washington Street, the main thoroughfare with broad sidewalks, banks, storefronts, and civic buildings, was all but lifeless. About the only remaining bit of vitality was the venerable Clam Broth House, a restaurant with a huge sign in the shape of a downward pointing hand.

Recently, I happened to find myself in Hoboken after not seeing it for a decade. What a difference 20 years can make. Old industrial buildings have been converted to loft housing. Scores of row houses have been renovated. New office buildings and condominiums had sprung up. Many new shops and cafes now lined the streets, along with a few espresso bars.

Thankfully, Hoboken has not been entirely gentrified. Some things are exactly the same. Laemmel's Pork Store is on the same corner where it has been for over 50 years. The little diner across from the train station serves up eggs and bacon for three dollars and change. And the Clam Broth House is still going strong, though it has been spiffed up.

Here in the Pacific Northwest, a similar transformation is taking place in Everett. While much has been made of Tacoma's rebirth, the changes taking place in Everett are no less amazing.

Many people know about the Navy Homeport, one of the few newly built naval bases in the country. However, because of all the news about it being on, then off, then on again, some may have gotten the impression that not much is

Designed by ZGF Architects, this new Navy Homeport complex exhibits a level of quality not seen for many decades in military buildings.

there, that the Navy still hasn't made a commitment to build it. Well, not only has the commitment been made, the base is complete.

And it is one of the most spectacular military installations that has been seen in many decades. It is necessary to reach back as far as the Presidio in San Francisco or Annapolis in Maryland to see anything with such a fine degree of design, from the grounds to the buildings.

The base is organized around a central pedestrian "spine" along which most of the buildings are aligned. A parallel street will carry a transit shuttle, as well as other vehicles.

No mean-spirited, austere "government" structures here. The first buildings—a police and fire station and a logistics center—served to set the level of quality for those that followed. Buildings must conform to guidelines that specify the use of red brick, contrasting belt courses near the ground, green metal sloped roofs, and vertically proportioned "punched" windows.

The one or two structures that somehow managed to escape these simple but effective rules are decidedly inferior. An exception is the system of bus shelters, made of glass and brightly painted steel. These exquisite little structures are finer than those seen in most urban transit systems.

The prominently located main administration building feels like a city hall in a small town. Although it has a somewhat confusing combination of forms (caused in part by a last-minute addition), it is nonetheless a splendid centerpiece.

However unexpectedly delightful the Navy base may be, the real action in

Everett is in the downtown. Just a few years ago, the place seemed to be dead. City and county buildings, along with a few interesting older structures, were adrift in a sea of vacant commercial buildings, marginal stores, and empty streets. A beautification project in the mid-'70s failed to produce any marked improvement in the health or appearance of the downtown. The one tangible result was that the city now has an inventory of magnificent street trees.

But, over the past few years, things have changed.

For its part, the city has been, for some years, quietly using a revolving loan fund called the "Community Housing Improvement Program," or CHIP. Dozens of older buildings within and around downtown have been given low-interest loans for renovation and repair. According to Dave Koenig of the city's planning department, "CHIP has accomplished a number of projects which demonstrate that the city cares about its downtown and has made a long-term commitment to its revival." Businesses responded. New enterprises, such as the excellent Pave bakery and the Passport restaurant opened and are thriving—even at night. CHIP helped with providing hundreds of units of housing for people with modest incomes. Some of these are found in the renovated upper floors of older commercial buildings.

The Snohomish County Public Utility District recently placed its new headquarters building in downtown, and Group Health put up a clinic and offices near the freeway. The old downtown library, with its art deco detailing, was remodeled and expanded. Everett High School, just outside the downtown, was restored to its former classic elegance.

Colby Crest is a complex of moderate-priced apartments and street level shops. And the old Monte Cristo Hotel—abandoned for many years—holds low-income housing, gallery and office space for the Everett Cultural Commission, and public meeting rooms. The lobby was restored to its former grandeur.

Michael Shopenn

GGLO Architects were responsible for designing the renovation of this abandoned hotel into housing for low-income people and space for social services.

The new Colby Square includes the Everett Community Theater. Whimsical glass pieces by Dale Chihuly adorn the lobby walls. Along Everett Avenue, the back side of the building, which would typically be blank, has windows opening into the scenery shops.

With such a fine civic building as the theater is, the city needs to give it a suitable forecourt. The '60s-era suburban style bank and parking lot that occupy the rest of the block should be acquired and made into a town square. Perhaps following the examples of Portland and Bellevue, a design competition could be held. Everett's downtown needs a grand public space for community events, festivals, outdoor music, and art.

Recently, Art Skotdal, an astute and long-time property owner, built his own home on top of his offices near the intersection of Colby and Hewitt. An elegant sliver of a building, it would not look out of place on a street in San Francisco. On the northeast corner, Skotdal erected a mixed use building. Colby Center is a sophisticated piece of deco-inspired architecture. The upper floors contain luxury housing set back behind terraces overlooking the bay.

Downtown Everett is definitely seeing the fruits of some wise, bold decisions by both public and private leaders. This is beginning to show itself in some unusual ways. A civic association, calling itself "FOREVERETT," has prompted the city to reinstall the original unique-to-Everett light fixtures that used to grace downtown streets. This "re-lighting" project serves as a powerful symbol that downtown Everett is well on its way back to being a true City Center.

PART

II

Building Neighborhoods

Denni Shefrin

In 1978, Charles Royer, a popular news anchorman for KING-TV, won the mayoral election in Seattle over Paul Schell, who was then the director of Seattle's Community Development Department. For a number of years, Schell had led the agency, which was responsible for downtown development, historic preservation, the distribution of federal block grant funds, and neighborhood planning. We are now enjoying the legacy left by that era.

During the 1970s, the City of Seattle became a model for many other communities in a number of areas. Pioneer Square was saved from plans to turn it into a huge parking area for the office core. The Pike Place Market was likewise kept intact and completely renovated. Distressed neighborhoods throughout the city were targeted for selected public investments as identified by residents, property owners, and merchants. These actions set in motion the revitalization of urban neighborhoods from undesirable pockets of poorly maintained buildings and streets into the splendid, highly prized places that they are today.

After losing the mayoral race, Paul Schell became a developer, heading a new division of the Weyerhaeuser Company called Cornerstone Development. With a small contingent of aggressive and enlightened project managers, Cornerstone built dense, urban residential buildings within downtown at a time when the common wisdom was that people preferred to live in single-family areas. For the first few years, the buildings sat largely empty. But eventually, consumer preferences changed, and folks started lining up to buy or rent these new kinds of homes.

Today, downtown Seattle is one of the most desirable places to live. It is lively, interesting, attractive, and relatively safe. There is now a full range of choices in the city from fine, quiet outlying neighborhoods to active, exciting inner neighborhoods. Commercial streets are lined with local shops, cafes, grocery stores, and the ubiquitous coffee bars.

And, the idea caught on elsewhere in the region. Kirkland is almost awash in new apartments and condominiums. Bellevue is seeing several neighborhoods emerge in its increasingly dense downtown. Even suburban Redmond, home of Microsoft, has witnessed mixed use development within its low rise downtown.

And, in 1997, Paul Schell was elected mayor, 20 years after he first ran for the job.

8

Fremont:
Center of the Universe

In one of their classic comedic films, the Marx Brothers rule a mythical country called Fredonia. The place is populated with amusing characters and abounds with visual and verbal jokes. People burst into singing the silly national anthem at the slightest provocation.

Here in Seattle, we have our own version of the free-spirited little country in the form of a similarly named place. Fremont is a neighborhood that serves as a three-dimensional, and somewhat twisted, metaphor for the entire region. It is scraggly and disheveled. It is scrappy and self-reliant. It is filled with folks who are ingeniously creative, gently gregarious, and completely goofy in their view of life.

As an urban neighborhood, Fremont is a microcosm of the city that surrounds it. It sits on the edge of a body of water—in this case, not a natural one, but a long, narrow, man-made canal linking freshwater Lake Union with saltwater Puget Sound. Packed into an area roughly 10 blocks by 10 blocks is a plethora of idiosyncratic shops and restaurants, office buildings and small manufacturing plants, warehouses and apartment houses, small houses and pocket parks.

Many streets in the district intersect with other streets at odd angles, creating triangular parcels occupied by triangular buildings. A lot of the stuff in Fremont is not particularly attractive and some of it is downright ramshackle in appearance. Some parts of it never seem to change, other seems to always be changing. Fremont has a messy vitality that is endlessly interesting.

At the intersection of Fremont Avenue North and Fremont Place—"ground zero"—a tiny traffic island sports a signpost not unlike many found in rural hamlets throughout the world. Wooden signs in the shape of arrows point to

Created by local artists Steve Badanes, Will Martin, Donna Walter and Ross Whitehead, this fantastical creature—the Fremont Troll—lives beneath the Aurora Avenue bridge and is a beloved symbol of the neighborhood.

various destinations, some nearby and some continents away. The pole itself is painted with the words "Center of the Universe" above an arrow that points downward.

Within a stone's throw of this self-mockingly arrogant indicator are dozens of other delightfully tongue-in-cheek objects and homegrown businesses. Fremont is like the court jester with the bell-tipped cap who keeps reminding the rest of us not to take ourselves too seriously.

One of the most enduring and endearing symbols of the neighborhood is a life-sized sculpture of a clutch of people huddled beneath the shelter of a long-gone trolley stop. "Waiting for the Interurban" is a reminder of the days when Fremont was a streetcar suburb. Tracks across the Fremont drawbridge offered a tenuous connection to the big city in the early part of the century. Local people frequently dress the sculptured figures in old clothes and hats and trim the platform with decorations to celebrate holidays and birthdays. A dog standing among the stock-still patrons has the face of a man, a joke by the artist on an irascible Fremont citizen.

But this sculpture is only one of several that reflect the community's quirky, multifaceted character. On the eastern edge of the neighborhood, hulking beneath a huge highway bridge that soars overhead is the Fremont

Troll. A head the size of a house peeks out from the dark cavernous space below the bridge. Its gnarled fingers clutch a full-size, upturned Volkswagen. So well-known is this piece of art that it was mentioned by name in a recent referendum to clearly indicate to voters a precise spot in the city.

At one acutely angled intersection is a huge bronze statue of Lenin striking one of his revolutionary, heroic poses. It was discovered in a Russian dump by a local resident after the dissolution of the Soviet Union. He had it shipped to Seattle and persuaded Fremont to adopt it. In a supreme bit of irony, Lenin's upraised arm welcomes people to a community that is, at once, one of the most wildly liberal in the region and a hotbed of small-scale, individual capitalism.

A block south of the former Communist leader is another odd object: a large rocket. Marking the corner occupied by a second hand store filled with bric-a-brac ranging from old magazines to a mummy, the rocket used to grace the roof of an army surplus store in downtown Seattle. Now far less militaristic, the neon-trimmed missile emits wisps of steam from its tail and is trimmed with lights during Christmas. A more fitting tribute to the end of the Cold War could scarcely be concocted.

Knitted into the streets and blocks that surround these other-worldly icons are a whole host of commercial and industrial enterprises. Tiny espresso bars jostle up next to antique stores. The Empty Space Theatre is perched above an art gallery and the Longshoreman's Daughter, a cafe that is part working class diner and part upscale restaurant. Across the street is a flatiron building occupied by the aptly named Triangle Tavern, its outdoor tables jammed into an artistically fenced-in area that is at the apex of the triangular lot.

The main intersection of Fremont is marked by Yak's Teriyaki, a diminutive cafe that has been there for decades. A few doors away, the relatively new Fremont News has as good a selection of newspapers and magazines as any newsstand in New York City. The Glamorama store is chock full of unusual tchotchkes and hip clothing. Around the corner, the coffee house called Still Life in Fremont dispenses comforting coffee drinks, pastries, and a living room-like ambiance. A block over, the PCC Natural Market sells politically and ecologically enlightened selections of foodstuffs.

An underground second-hand store seems like a catacombs with its endless rabbit warren of cubicles crammed with old toys, jewelry, lamps, and retro clothing. A truly prized antique might be leaning against a true piece of junk—sort of like the neighborhood itself.

Surrounding the core of small businesses is an amazing array of things. A shoemaker sits next to a sail maker. A foundry is down the street from a brewery. Pubs share the same block with contractor's yards. This melange combines aspects of a Third World shantytown with an upscale urban shopping district. The neighborhood hosts a Sunday Market that draws people from throughout the metropolitan area to check out its offbeat items for sale. On warm summer nights, a parking lot is transformed into an outdoor cinema, much like those found in Italian towns. It all seems to work, and it gets more expansive and intricate with time.

One test of Fremont's resilience is to be found in the recent addition of a sprawling complex of buildings for the Adobe Systems software company. The architects drew from some of the features of the neighborhood—brick, metal siding, and vertically proportioned windows—and incorporated them into the buildings. But the sheer size and mass of the structures, together with repetitive windows, still smacks of a suburban office park. At least the windows are not bands of mirrored glass.

Fremont is a vivid demonstration of some of the best attributes of this region. It shows that we can accommodate change while maintaining a home-grown, one-of-kind character. It illustrates how to temper global economic influences with spontaneous and friendly face-to-face interaction. And it represents what great urban neighborhoods have always offered.

9

Neighborhoods Regained

From time to time during my life, I have felt like the title character in the Woody Allen film *Zelig* who happens to be in the background of momentous events. One of those times for me was being in Moscow in 1991, in the days immediately following the attempted coup, when the Soviet Union was visibly dissolving hour by hour.

But the most electrifying instance was in 1968. Departing the University of Oklahoma slightly before spring break officially began, I spent most of the day on Thursday, April 4, driving from Norman to Memphis, Tennessee. I had an interview on Friday with an architectural firm in that city for a summer job.

Arriving late in the afternoon, I immediately became lost in the unfamiliar maze of downtown streets. A little after 6 p.m., I turned down Mulberry Street. Suddenly, people were rushing about—frantic, confused, and angry. Police and ambulance sirens approached from all directions.

Though I soon turned out of the area, I found out later that evening that I had been a few dozen feet from where Martin Luther King, Jr., had just been murdered on the balcony of the Lorraine Motel. In the days that followed, the city was locked down. A rigid curfew was imposed. Troop trucks and tanks of the Tennessee National Guard would rumble past my window.

Martin Luther King knew the power that words have to affect people. His writings and his speeches were both eloquent and galvanizing. That is why I find the monument to Dr. King here in Seattle, on Martin Luther King Way and South Walker, so disappointing. This is certainly not to denigrate the fine efforts of the many people and organizations that helped establish this memorial. But it seems crude and simplistic. The static, mountain-like monument, referring to King's famous speech, seems more off-putting than engaging. Other memorials to King, such as the one in San Francisco, are much more powerful.

Perhaps a more dramatic tribute to King's ideals and dreams is found in the neighborhoods around the monument. After decades of being torn apart by property acquisition and construction of Interstate 90, these neighborhoods are finally beginning to heal.

The most expansive project is the park that has been built on top of the lid that conceals the freeway as it penetrates the Mount Baker neighborhood. The park contains some elements that are extraordinarily beautiful. Other aspects, however, are mundane.

On the former end of the spectrum, the shafts and structures that provide ventilation for the freeway tunnel are enormous but are stepped and slightly angled back. They convey a raw power amidst the landscape that surrounds them. Lacy metal grillwork adds an unexpectedly light touch.

A succession of gradually rising, cryptic rock forms flank the main promenade for walkers and bicyclists. This formidable piece of public art was done by artists Keith Blakely and Dennis Evans. Another piece is the "Waterworks," located unexpectedly within a stormwater drainage basin. Designed by artists Carl Chew and Ellen Zeigler, it combines fact and fiction.

What is truly unfortunate about this park is the missed opportunity that it represents.

It might have been a great piece of open space, with outdoor rooms shaped by walls of closely spaced trees. It could have contained an outdoor performance space, with grassy terraces. Instead, the shapes and forms that are there add up to little in the way of true urban character. The place feels like just a bunch of leftover landscaping. Ironically, a striking, almost poetic design for the park was developed in the early '80s—and subsequently watered down by budget-cutting bureaucrats in the state Department of Transportation.

Throughout the park, there are a number of very strange things. In one area, an elegant staircase, with well-crafted handrails can be found, while 50 feet away plain, bent-pipe handrails have been slapped into a crudely finished flight of steps. A long, wide raised planter is almost, but not quite, on axis with the pedestrian tunnel. The parapet walls near the entrance to this tunnel are topped with (hopefully temporary) pipes that lean to and fro with strands of twisted wire connecting them.

Perhaps the most absurd touch is a large, totally empty, lighted parking lot that might be used by the public were it not cordoned off by a thick steel cable. Clearly, this park needs some design attention

On the positive side, the new Colman Elementary School sits on the north side of the park. Incorporating brick and gabled roof forms, it elegantly recalls the old Colman school on the other side of the park. The new school is an exemplary piece of architecture that should set the level of quality for other public and private buildings to follow.

The old school is slated to become an African American Heritage Museum and Cultural Center. Offering interpretive exhibits, a visual arts center, and performing arts spaces, the center will make an important contribution to the area. Once restored, this building, with its colorful history, should serve as a dignified and dramatic landmark.

A few blocks south of the park, on Martin Luther King Way, is a tiny building that could easily be missed. Housing the private, nonprofit Central Youth and Family Services, it demonstrates that even a facility on a tight budget can have fine architecture. The building skillfully incorporates concrete block, corrugated metal, and other industrial materials in crisp, bold forms.

Some distance to the south is the historic Franklin High School. Reopened a few years ago, after extensive repair and renovation, Franklin High is nothing less than magnificent. The sloped floor theater and arch-windowed commons room make superb venues for live musical and theatrical performances. But saving this structure was hardly an easy task. The school district insisted upon tearing it down, saying it was too costly to maintain. Other heads prevailed; a group of architects and preservation advocates did an extensive analysis demonstrating that renovating and restoring the grand old school was actually more cost-effective than building a new one.

The symbolic importance to surrounding neighborhoods of keeping this school intact cannot not be measured. It has spurred an active reinvestment in the area by dozens of groups, institutions, and businesses. In the past few years, many vacant lots have been purchased and hundreds of new homes for low- and moderate-income households have been constructed.

Now that the dust has settled, new commercial investment is expected along the Rainier Avenue corridor. Already, a large complex of new neighborhood stores was built in the Genesee district. New businesses, many owned by Vietnamese families, have moved into buildings along the avenue.

All in all, this is a neighborhood that has rediscovered itself.

10

Three New Business Districts

In the last 15 years, something quite wonderful happened in Seattle. While we weren't looking, we picked up three new business districts. Appearing from virtually nowhere, these districts are the "Madison Valley," what might be called "Upper Madison," and "Little Saigon."

That these places exist is remarkable for several reasons. Usually it takes many years, if not decades, for commercial streets to emerge and mature. Streets like Broadway, 45th Street, and Market Street have long histories of being built, changing, evolving, being refined.

These new districts have been principally the result of actions by a handful of people and businesses who saw opportunities, took risks, and forged ahead undaunted by the odds against their success. The city has appeared to do little in the way of encouragement or reinforcement, other than adopting zoning laws to permit it all to happen. After all, no law can force people to open and operate a business. There must be a demand and someone who is ready to fill it.

The Madison Valley appeared first, popping up in the early '80s along a forlorn stretch of Madison Street between 27th Avenue and the Washington Park Arboretum. That stretch of street had been lined with decrepit buildings and trash-strewn vacant lots. Now the district is filled with buildings, shops, cafes, and apartments. There is even a landmark building, in the form of the Bailey-Boushay House, a hospice for AIDS patients.

The similarity of buildings along the street is no coincidence. Ten of them were designed and built by Charles "Bud" Bergmann, an architect who forged out on his own after working for other well-known architects around town. Small, two- and three-story stucco-faced structures, they embrace the street with storefronts, awnings, and signs scaled to people on foot rather than in cars. Some have courtyards leading to offices and apartments in the rear or above.

With some help from an enlightened banker, a progressive thinking insurance agent, and some brave co-investors, Bergmann began buying up properties, renovating, expanding, or building one block at a time. As he proceeded, other folks came in. The owners of City People's Mercantile purchased the rundown garden store at the east end of the district and transformed it into the City People's Nursery.

Few buildings stand out, but that is the strength of this district: The effect is that of a finely tuned orchestra. The resulting composition is in the fine, but almost lost, traditions of building quiet little business districts in which the buildings are well-mannered and unobtrusive. The street feels comfortable, intimate, and lively.

Walking along Madison in this stretch now, it is hard to imagine that it was anything other than a splendid little pocket of urbanity.

The second new district is also along Madison Street in what might be called "Upper Madison," between Terry and Boylston, in the middle of the First Hill

Mark Hinshaw

Upper Madison is a lively new urban neighborhood, anchored by major hospitals.

neighborhood. The district has a fine collection of stately older buildings such as the Sorrento Hotel, the Gainsborough, and 1223 Spring Street, all of which sport fanciful rooftops.

For decades, the district was slowly being chewed up by the expansion of health care institutions and number of rudely scaled residential towers. But finally, Upper Madison is beginning to come together. Enough pieces are falling into place to suggest that the district is well on the way to being a pretty fine neighborhood business district.

Recently, Swedish Hospital has included storefronts along the street as it has added new buildings. They have been filled with needed cafes, drugstores, and services. The facade along the eastern wing is a bit bloated with enormous, clumsily proportioned columns. The colonnade is too high at one end and too low at the other and principally serves to block views of the storefronts from the street.

Even the store signs are barely visible, set high above and parallel to the curb. Only people directly across the street have any hope of seeing them. Nevertheless, on a recent warm day, spaces between the columns were filled with tables and chairs and people.

The recently completed west wing demonstrates how to do street-facing shops the right way. The facade includes well-proportioned windows and decorative details. Elegantly curved canopies project out from the wall, protecting people from the rain without blocking visibility of the showcase windows. Signs are often placed inside windows and give off a warm glow at night.

The extra wide sidewalk allows for a long row of cafe tables and chairs. The drugstore window is pretty boring, but that is not the fault of the designers. Someone needs to offer to managers of drug stores a course on interesting methods of displaying signs and merchandise.

One of the new tenants is Torino's—the first of many cafes to be built by the family-owned company that has been making sausage for over 60 years. The cafe and deli is neat, cozy, and well-appointed, with gorgeous displays of pasta and Italian sandwiches.

Across the street, McDonald's recently gave itself a makeover. While it's better than many, it is still pretty mundane. But the prize for the worst facade has to go the U.S. Bank. A huge, ungainly white brick box, it has a nonsensical arch set behind a barren apron of asphalt. If the bank has to have a parking lot along the street, it need only look at its neighbor to the east.

There, Key Bank is housed in a finely scaled, masonry building that might be found in a small town. Its L-shaped form joins up with the sidewalk and has a welcoming entry. There is a parking lot, but it is tucked off to the side and holds two massive trees.

To the east of Key Bank is First Hill Plaza—a tower of extraordinary dullness. It hardly looks like a place where people live; it might be a hotel or perhaps an office building. At least the ground level gives something to the street, though even here, the split-level sidewalk is pretty strange. After a series of tenants that came and disappeared, the complex is finely getting some decent shops.

While Upper Madison is not as lively, as intimate, or as diverse as other districts, it could grow into something very fine. One thing that would help is if the city could put together a project to add street trees and decorative lights.

Little Saigon is awash in lively signs and small, family-owned shops.

The third district is a new concentration of food markets, restaurants, shops, and services that has rapidly expanded around the intersection of 12th and Jackson. Now known as Little Saigon, it is a wonderfully chaotic crazy quilt of buildings, signs, people, and merchandise—much like the wildly exuberant atmosphere found in commercial districts of many cities and towns in Asian countries.

For the moment, the centerpiece of the district is the pleasant, three-story complex of a market and shops called the Ding How Shopping Center. A wing of the complex wraps around the corner and faces 12th. The market is spotless and well lighted, displays an astonishing array of fish, and sells French bread as fine as can be found in Paris.

Hiep Quach, a local banker who moved to Seattle 30 years ago, explains that many of the merchants originally came to the U.S. as "boat people" in the early '80s. Because it has been seen as a desirable place to live, Seattle now has one of the largest concentrations of Vietnamese in the country. Little Saigon is seen as a major location for Vietnamese to socialize as well as attend to shopping needs. Says Hiep: "Vietnamese love to eat."

Indeed, on a recent Saturday, most of the cafes and restaurants were packed. Cars were queued up to get into parking lots. For now, the district is pretty much a commercial center. But as the local Vietnamese population matures, housing may start to crop up around the edges, transforming it into a real urban neighborhood.

Even without new housing, the energy and enterprise seen in Little Saigon could be reinforced by some enlightened application of public investment. This could come in the form of art, sidewalk enhancements, or public spaces. But please, let's not make it pretty. The messy vitality is magnificent.

11

Institutions That Build Good Neighborhoods

There is an old joke in certain circles that goes like this: "India has a caste system. England has a class system. And America has zoning." As with any bit of biting humor, this holds some amount of truth.

One of the terrible legacies of the early 20th century is the notion that single-family houses must be protected, at all costs, from every other form of development. This idea originated around the end of the 1800s when unfettered industrialization resulted in numerous social ills. Back then it was not uncommon to find animal rendering plants and steel mills cheek by jowl with the houses of the people who worked there. Despite the romantic image that we tend to have of the turn of the century, conditions were pretty awful. Many people died from tuberculosis, caused or exacerbated by foul air. Drinking water was tainted by untreated human waste and chemical effluence.

Separating residential land uses from industry was advanced as one way of improving human health and welfare. Eventually, this simple idea was transformed into that of placing all land uses into discrete "zones." Over the course of several decades, neighborhoods were stripped of local stores. Cottage industries were given the boot. Denser forms of housing were viewed with disdain. And institutions were banished to the least desirable parts of town. By the 1950s, single-purpose zoning was firmly entrenched in the country's legal and political system. Unfortunately, our penchant for separating land uses and spreading them out across the landscape has contributed to traffic congestion, degradation of air quality, destruction of forests, farmlands, and wetlands, and fiscal strife in local government.

Zoning has frequently served to reinforce the xenophobic attitudes of some people. Many local laws have been passed in the name of public health and safety, but in fact they were thinly veiled attempts at racial, social, or economic segregation. Even institutions with the noble purpose of providing services and care to ill or less able-bodied people have been seen as undesirable. And when built, they frequently have been austere, antiseptic, and even downright ugly, attributes that merely reinforce the perception that they are unsuited to be located within a neighborhood.

It is remarkable, then, that any specialized institution can be built at all today within a neighborhood setting. It is astonishing when such an institution actually contributes to the character of its surroundings.

Two Seattle neighborhoods have been enhanced by the development of unique institutions in their midst. The facilities are stellar examples of buildings that serve both their clientele and their surroundings with skill, sensitivity, and a high level of style.

The Boyer Children's Clinic in the Montlake neighborhood was built on the site of a previous clinic. The increased amount of floor area and state of the art equipment allows for a full complement of programs that are devoted to children with cerebral palsy and delays in development. While its interior is outfitted with comfortable finishes and furnishings, as well as wonderful artwork, its exterior exhibits an extraordinary fit with the surrounding context.

The architects employed design elements with a distinctly residential imagery. They fused together forms and materials that echo those found elsewhere in this neighborhood of stately houses. The brick facade contains vertically proportioned windows with wide white trim. The pitched roof form of the building repeats the pattern established along the street. Even the setbacks match almost precisely those of the nearby residential structures. A projecting, visually prominent "turret" completes the composition, adding a touch of elegance that is almost never seen in institutions, especially a small one on a tight budget.

A considerable effort was made to assure neighbors that the new building would respect the character of the area. The result is a place that is uplifting in spirit and a dramatic demonstration that institutions can be an integral part of a neighborhood.

In the Madison Valley is the Bailey-Boushay House, built to house people with AIDS. The planning and development of this institution was at times almost consumed by controversy. While it had strong supporters, it also has a number of very vocal and persistent opponents. Its construction commenced only after a settlement was reached.

Now that the Bailey-Boushay House has been open for a while, it appears to have made a positive contribution to the scale, texture, and diversity of the emerging district. The Bailey-Boushay House is a finely crafted building with a landmark quality. Although it has rather common materials—concrete block

Mark Hinshaw

The Bailey-Bouschee House, an AIDS Hospice designed by the Bumgardner architects, serves as the dignified centerpiece of its neighborhood.

and stucco—the building is so well detailed that it presents a graceful face to the community.

Masonry belt courses anchor the building's street face, and ground-level windows are detailed like storefronts. The floors above read like small apartments, with a repeated gable providing a symbol of "home." An octagonal cupola form prominently located at the corner contains a sun-filled greenhouse and serves as a "marker" for the district, something that it previously lacked.

Both of these fine buildings remind us that we are a society and a community with many different types of people, some of which need special care and attention. No one should be shoved out of sight just because they have unusual needs. Every neighborhood should be looking for ways to comfortably accommodate small-scale institutions such as these. As a result, we will all be better off.

12

The Tragedy of The Commons

Unlike many large cities in North America, Seattle has never embraced big urban redevelopment projects. Portland has an urban renewal district that gave it a dense neighborhood on the edge of downtown. San Francisco worked for 30 years on the Yerba Buena project, which is now filled with the Moscone Convention Center, art museums, hotels, shops, and open spaces. Baltimore transformed its waterfront through its massive Inner Harbor project. Vancouver built a new town along False Creek, anchored by the immensely popular Granville Island Market. Similarly, scores of other cities have assembled big chunks of land and charged ahead with ambitious development plans

But not Seattle.

The quality, character, and quirkiness of this city is the result of thousands of decisions by individuals, organizations, corporations, and government agencies. Rarely has any one person, group, or government entity been able to call the shots.

Seattle is a great city precisely because it is a rich melange of distinct, different and sometimes disparate pieces. It is a lovingly crafted quilt—odd bits of fabric sewn together over years of time into an exquisitely eccentric, bumpy blanket. It gets its greatness not through grand civic gestures, but from the sum of small accretions that lie cheek by jowl, swirling paisley against plain plaid.

In the early 1990s, a number of influential people began pushing a proposal for The Commons, a grand new park at the north end of downtown. Though well meaning and enthusiastic, they did not seem to understand the idea's fundamental flaw. It was simply too big, too expensive, too demanding, too overwhelming. It symbolized a style of city building that smacked of a clear-it-away-and-start-over-again attitude that goes against our basic grain. Consequently the ballot proposal to fund it lost heavily at the polls.

The notion of making major public investments to revitalize this neighborhood is still valid. We should infuse the center of the city with greenery and gardens. This builds upon our fine heritage of greenbelts, boulevards, parks, and promenades. City dwellers we may be, but we still want to see and touch things that grow.

Many of the businesses now found in the area could well remain as tenants in new buildings, though perhaps with a different form of operation. Van Ness Avenue in the heart of San Francisco is surrounded by housing but is still lined with car dealerships, although they are located inside multi-story structures. Portland's Pearl District is home to a wide array of printing companies, photo labs, business supply companies, and wholesalers that serve the downtown.

Streets within the neighborhood should not be given over to high-priced boutiques, and trendy cafes. The place must be a real neighborhood—blending gritty humanity, bustling commerce, and pleasant places to live. The area should accommodate a good measure of messiness and eccentricity.

All cities change over time. Businesses come and go, expand and move. Some disappear; others reappear in a different form. A street that is lined with warehouses in one generation may be bustling with shops in the next. That is what makes cities so intriguing and lively.

Finally, this potential new neighborhood also offers an opportunity to finally have a place to celebrate and explain an important part of our heritage. For over 20 years, many people have been working on putting a collection of ships and interpretive displays at the south end of Lake Union. Although the schooner Wawona is moored there already and the Center for Wooden Boats is certainly fine, Seattle deserves to have a first class museum of maritime history.

Commerce crossed with culture. Places to work mixed with places to live. These are what great urban neighborhoods are all about.

13

Tacoma Turns Itself Around

It has been interesting to watch the cities of Seattle and Tacoma wrestle with how to strengthen and enhance their neighborhoods. So far, Tacoma has Seattle beat by a long shot.

The bigger city has been putting its neighborhood folks though seemingly endless meetings and workshops, "Phase 1" plans and "Phase 2" plans, settings goals, making lists, filling out surveys, hiring "facilitators" to organize meetings and designers to draw spiffy drawings. Tacoma, on the other hand, has been spending its energy and money actually making tangible improvements.

Throughout Tacoma, whole sections of the community are seeing infusions of capital, both public and private, that are bringing in new public spaces, civic amenities, and sidewalks, trails, and vastly improved local shopping districts. The commitment and tenacity of many people—elected leaders, government officials, business people, and residents—is remarkable. There is a genuine spirit of collaboration, cooperation, and creativity.

The south end of downtown is rapidly being transformed by the development of the branch campus for the University of Washington. The renovation of older, formerly languishing industrial buildings is adding to the fine collection of splendid new and historic buildings in the area, including the Union Station/Court House and the adjacent State Historical Museum. The theater district at Broadway and 9th is a terrific mix of old and new, right next to the landscaped plaza of a bustling new transit center.

The Tacoma Dome district is coming alive with the gloriously funky Freighthouse packed with odd shops and ethnic cafes. A new bus transit center has been completed. Eventually this district will have a light rail connection into the heart of downtown.

Along the city's north shore is a two-mile-long boulevard and esplanade

Courtesy of LMN Architects

Downtown Tacoma is the home of a new branch campus for the University of Washington. Architects Moore Ruble Yudell in association with LMN Architects designed the campus to fit within a group of former industrial buildings.

embellished with planting, public art, and pocket parks overlooking Commencement Bay. Old Town is getting livelier each month with new eateries and nearby housing.

Perhaps the most remarkable change in Tacoma has taken place in the relatively tiny neighborhood business district at 26th Avenue North and Proctor. A few years ago, this six-block district was little more than an incidental crossroads with smattering of stores that seemed to be barely hanging on. Today, it is a lively, attractive miniature downtown, with markets, coffee bars, sidewalk cafes, specialty shops, nightlife, and ethnic restaurants.

Pomodoro, a new Northern Italian restaurant, is packed every night. Its sophisticated, European-style bistro windows fold back in mild weather so that diners become part of the street scene. Joe Quilici, the restaurant's ebullient owner, retired from the city Planning Department after putting in his 30 years and decided to give something back to the community. He and his wife, Judy, who owns a nearby shop, are articulate advocates for the neighborhood.

But many, many local people played key roles in the rejuvenation of the place. Bill Evans provided some early new investment by buying an old Victorian house and converting it to an elegant gift shop and cafe. Recently, he sold the cafe portion to his employees, but his wife continues to run the store.

Across the street is Evans's "Pacific Northwest" shop, brimming with all manner of local comestibles and clothing.

Prior to making his investment moves, Evans spent a lot of his own time traveling around the country and observing what worked in other places. Astute and aggressive, he is constantly marketing the district to prospective merchants and financial institutions. This is one neighborhood person who won't settle for mere talk; he puts his money where his mouth is.

Likewise, local architect Gene Grulich has contributed both his talent and his resources to turning this area around. With a group of friends, he purchased the old Blue Mouse Theater, restored it, and found an operator to bring in a combination of contemporary art films and classic silent movies. He provided design services to shop owners along the street, detailing sensitive renovations under a city-sponsored program that offers architects "on call." The city also helps business owners secure low-interest loans for renovation work.

The results are impressive. The elegant Jasminka, a store that has been in the neighborhood for 15 years, now looks like it could be on a side street in Paris. Other business owners have renovated their stores. Safeway updated a tired old store by adding expansive, well-detailed windows and bringing its sign down to human scale. Across the street, the new Thriftway is composed of a combination of storefronts topped by a large, artfully designed logo.

And the city has done its own part with some simple but effective enhancements. Sidewalks have been replaced with fresh concrete. Street trees enclosed in decorative, wrought iron fencing were planted along the sidewalks. Pleasant benches, trash containers, and bike racks were installed. Local artist Paul Michaels was commissioned to embed bronze bas-reliefs into the surface of the sidewalk. They explain the colorful, but almost forgotten, history of the district.

While an obligatory Starbucks occupies one of the prime corners, its presence is certainly a significant sign that this is a place that is alive. Indeed, its sidewalk tables are almost always full of locals. Here shop keepers know their customers, greeting them by their first names. And even more remarkable is the fact that this is not a haven just for well-heeled yuppies or body-pierced Gen-Xers. Families, singles, seniors, and young adults commingle and converse. This is a place where the ultra-hip Bulldog News is a few steps away from Julia Ellen's dress shop and around the corner from venerable Henry's Bakery.

Grulich attributes the positive change in the district to "many little successes over years of time and by a lot of different people." This is the real lesson for other cities. Community groups can get impatient, hoping for the big government grant, or the next beneficent corporation, or a hoped-for new park as the singular solution to their needs. Worse, far too many neighborhood folks place the entire burden on the private sector to shake loose some of their "excess profits." Waiting around for any of these things wastes time and wastes energy.

The homily may be trite, but it is true: "You got to walk the walk, not just talk the talk." Tacoma is showing us all how to walk.

III

Streets That Work

Denni Shefrin

Not long ago if someone in Seattle wanted to enjoy a bit of bohemian street life it was necessary to buy a ticket to San Francisco. Now there are so many different and lively streets in Citistate Seattle that they have taken on highly individualized characteristics.

Broadway in the Capitol Hill neighborhood is the center of pierced and tattooed body parts. A stroll along that 10-block-long street is marked by youthful crowds jostling to get into the latest trendy clothing store. Intersecting Broadway are the parallel streets of East Pike and East Pine. Sidewalks are lined with cafes, lounges, dance clubs, and bric-a-brac shops catering to a largely gay population.

The east end of Madison Street, before it ends in Lake Washington, has a big clutch of stores and restaurants aimed at the distinctly upscale neighborhood. Cafes spill out onto the sidewalk. On Sunday morning, local residents queue up at their favorite breakfast spots.

Downtown, First Avenue is alive with nightspots and cool clothing stores. The recently opened Pampas Room features floor shows and dancing. Smartly dressed couples swirl about the dimly lighted art deco floor like dancers in a Busby Berkeley musical. A few blocks away, singles dressed in black lounge at the Lux—a dark espresso bar decorated in high rococo.

The "cafe society" phenomenon has even hit the suburbs. Kirkland's downtown streets are filled with people strolling to and from a myriad of restaurants and nightspots. Redmond Town Center teems with young people. We now enjoy the multiple choices and chance encounters that good streets have always offered.

14

An Avenue Becomes a Street

For several years in the mid-'90s, I leased a small office on Western Avenue. One day, I dropped into a computer store to purchase a few accessories for my laptop. Gillian, the salesperson, typed my name and address into the PC on the counter. "Oooh," she said as she typed the street, "Western is the coolest street in town." Then she went on to describe its chief attributes. "It has so many shops and restaurants, lots of different people, and some neat buildings."

Actually, I had not really thought of it as "cool." Rather, my image of it seemed to be rooted in its earlier days. Hardly more than a wide alley, Western was really in the backwater, caught between the bustle of the harbor and the high rise energy of downtown. For many years, its character was dominated by parking lots lying in the shadows of soaring concrete overpasses. Even the portion that wrapped around the Pike Place Market seemed oddly dead. One of my first and lasting impressions of initially visiting Seattle was the long, vertiginous, uninterrupted stair that used to lead from the quietude of Western Avenue up to the cacophony of Pike Place.

But the new Western Avenue is as Gillian described. Along most of its 1.5 miles, from Yesler to where it dissolves into Elliott, there is an amazing array of stuff. It has some of the city's newest, niftiest buildings and some of its oldest and most mundane. Only 15 years ago, the pioneering Hillclimb Court seemed to be going unsold. Now, the avenue is lined with housing. And not just of the luxurious sort either. There is everything from tony-view condominiums to low-income apartments to rock-bottom residential hotels. Amazingly, there is still a tiny clutch of old wood frame houses hidden behind some overgrown vegetation.

In the last few years, Western has been invaded by a host of new people and businesses. Architects and landscape architects, artists and graphic designers, printers and publishers, have creatively filled spaces in a number of old loft

Most of the older warehouse buildings along Western have been renovated into loft-style space while newer mixed-use buildings have been added.

Denni Shefrin

buildings. The result is not unlike the early days of SoHo in New York City.

The legendary Wild Ginger restaurant is on Western. There are antique stores, high style furniture shops, a place that hawks parrots, a brewery, and a French bakery. The Millionaire's Club always has, at the ready, a cadre of out-of-work laborers eagerly awaiting their early morning pick up by customers. There are even a couple of children's play areas tucked onto the rooftops above the street.

A Business Improvement Association has taken on the responsibility for picking up loose trash, nighttime security, and the installation of wall art. The huge leaping whale near University Street is part of a large, multi-paneled piece that wraps around the corner of an otherwise ordinary building.

For the most part, all of this density and diversity is packed into buildings no more than six stories high. The street is safe, it is lively, it is livable, and it is attractive. But cute it is not; there is traffic and congestion. Trucks lurch about, evidence of a working city.

So, what makes this corridor work? As it turns out, only a handful of ingredients are responsible for the marvelous stew that results.

First, there is effectively no "zoning." Of course, there are height limits and design standards to protect the historic character. Other than that, almost anything can be found on the avenue. Residential buildings peacefully coexist with warehouses and bulk retail. There are steam plants and substations down the way from elegant shops. Late into the evening on weekends, the clopping sound of horses slowly pulling polished carriages reverberates off the walls. Their stable is also on the street, as is the odoriferous product of their digestive process.

With all its variety, Western Avenue has a great degree of continuity. There are very few open lots that break the line of buildings. The right-of-way is narrower than other downtown streets. This slender envelope of space—60 feet wide rather than the more typical 80—is a crucial factor. Combined with wide sidewalks, parked cars, occasional street trees, and two relatively narrow traffic lanes, it produces a very pleasant, almost intimate, urban corridor.

Few buildings along Western are anything to write home about. The collective whole is more far important than individual parts. This, then, is the best of urban design. No one gets to shout and no one needs to be ashamed of something that's just doing a decent job.

There is, perhaps, one design principle that has served this street exceedingly well: Storage space for cars, though abundantly available, is rarely visually prominent. Most parking in recent years has been placed below, behind, or above street level shops. Even the few truly identifiable garages have either shallow shopfronts (as at Western and Seneca) or whimsical metal artwork (as at the "Alexandria" near Denny).

Storefronts along the street are done exactly the way they should be: generous expanses of glass, high bays, a substantial sill line, wood casing and mullions—qualities so simple to produce and humane in their effect that it is incredible that we have spent the past 50 years *not* doing these things on our retail streets. For hundreds of years, we intuitively knew how to do shopfronts well; somewhere along the way, we just seemed to forget. It is instructive that the only building that has had a tough time attracting and keeping retail tenants is the only one that does not adhere to these rules.

Down on Yesler, a tiny brick building lists against what has to be one of the smallest, but most precious, residential courtyards anywhere this side of Paris. Sometimes you can see, at seven o'clock in the morning, when the big doors of the tiny building are open, the blinding spray of sparks from an arc welder—only feet from the bedrooms of nearby homes. This is "mixed use" at its most extreme. Not for everyone's taste, perhaps, but plenty of people are paying good money for the privilege of being amidst it all. One of the tragedies of the late 20th century is that those who cringe at these seemingly incongruous activities have projected their biases onto everyone else. This attitude has dominated public policy for so many years that we have almost banished lively combinations of human activity out of existence.

Streets like Western Avenue sing with the life of the city. The place is as intriguing at 12 midnight as it is at 12 noon. Western probably will never be called a really "great" street. No matter. It represents what good cities have always offered: density, diversity, and conviviality—urbanity at its very best.

15

Espresso al Fresco

A few years ago, I walked up to the little sidewalk stand and plunked down a few bills and several coins to purchase a large cup of brown liquid. Taking in a big sip, I was immediately taken by an impulse to heave it up into the nearby gutter. Nothing that ever landed on my tongue had tasted quite so ghastly.

A nightmarish experience at an off-brand espresso vendor using sour milk? No. The stand was selling *kvas* on a street corner in Moscow. This dreadful drink, as popular in that city as lattes are to us, is made from fermented bread, and tastes like, well, liquid bread. Not only did the taste give me the urge to lose my lunch, but it was served up in a common, and clearly unwashed, glass. A few days later, I had a full case of Lenin's revenge.

Kvas obviously is a culturally acquired taste. Like our espresso stands, kvas kiosks are found throughout Moscow. They are one of the things that tell you that you are definitely in the capital city of Russia. A number of major cities throughout the world have their own little unique sidewalk symbols.

Paris has its bouquinistes, purveying books, posters, and assorted bric-a-brac. In New York, the hot dog carts sell something that visually resembles frankfurters, but is really, I suspect, a novel way of disposing of toxic waste. Tokyo streets are lined with little noodle shops, their thin cloth banners providing the only separation between customers' backs and passersby. In similar fashion, the image of Citistate Seattle is now partly defined by the presence of espresso stands.

Sure, we have had coffeehouses and coffee bars for several decades now. But it is the wheeled carts and the free-standing roadside kiosks that have sprung up by the hundreds over the past 10 years that now give us a character that is unlike most other places in the country.

Some of the folks who run these places really have caught on to their potential to create little oases along otherwise hard-edged streets. Their stands or

Diane Mucci's espresso cart is one of the best of the many hundreds in the city.

carts are occasionally labors of love with carefully chosen color schemes, great graphics, and elegant furnishings. A few permanent stands have added landscaping, tables, and decks. These are wonderful little bits of urban design, crafted by hand and fitted into their surroundings.

Whether I'm in the mood for coffee or not, I always glance at the Commuter Comforts kiosk near the ferry terminal on Bainbridge Island. It is a visual treat and the owner always keeps it as neat as a pin. Likewise, the little hole-in-the-wall of Just Say Espresso in Ballard is attractive and immaculate.

While Starbucks, SBC, and Tully's give us snazzy corporate interiors and graphic design, it is remarkable to see so many small scale entrepreneurs do an exemplary job of combining service with style. Often, the efforts of individual merchants are far more homey. Certainly they are more free-spirited.

As gas stations gradually disappear from streets, they are being replaced by espresso stands. Along some busy arterials, they seem to be at every intersection. Like the roadside diners of an earlier era, they often announce themselves with a distinctive design. The Espresso Connection stand at 47th and Evergreen Way in Everett presents a welcome relief to the unrelenting swath of car lots and discount stores. This little kiosk is nicely proportioned and topped with globe lights. There is a plaza outfitted with tables and chairs right on the corner.

Down in the city of Des Moines, Debra Dapelo's stand occupies a tiny cottage-like structure that once held a watch shop. She has installed a delightful patio out front, complete with plants and hanging flower baskets. The atmosphere indicates that the owner is as much interested in contributing to the community image as running a business.

Throughout Seattle, there are now scores of coffee carts occupying sidewalks, plazas, and entrances to stores. One of the most interesting is Espresso di Mucci located at the entrance court of the Norton Building. Here a basic cart has been embellished with decorative wing panels and an elegant umbrella. A clutch of high-tech chairs and tables adds a sophisticated touch to the well-landscaped public space. When it rains, Diana Mucci pulls her cart through an opening in a bower of ivy and into an arcade along the building's facade.

Bulldog News combines espresso with magazines and newspapers from around the world.

Perhaps the best-designed stand in the city is not actually a free-standing one. But, it embraces the sidewalk in a similar way. The stand at Bulldog News on University Way faces both inward and outward. A simple awning with the logo announces the place from a distance, while the counter top is fully open to the people walking by. The combination of two stimulants—magazines and caffeine—is exquisite.

16

Potties for Pedestrians

Compared with many other North American cities, some areas of Seattle's downtown are lively. The streets and alleys in Pike Place Market comprise an energetic concentration of vitality, individuality, and quirkiness. Belltown streets are bursting with trendy shops, high-style restaurants, and nightlife. Pioneer Square, despite ups and downs, still holds its own as a lively district of art galleries, upscale eateries, and venues for live music. And the retail core is in the midst of rebuilding itself into a vibrant vortex of fashion, culture, and entertainment.

But despite these positive attributes, most of the sidewalks in downtown are downright dreary. With the exception of what was done to Fifth Avenue 20 years ago, the most important component of public space has little to commend it. Even the recently completed improvements along Pine Street are pretty bland. Can't we do something more than scored concrete walkways planted with a few trees and decorative light poles?

Behavioral researchers who have observed people walking in cities conclude that the liveliest places are those that offer the greatest number of choices: to sit, schmooze, lean, eat, watch other people, pick up a magazine or newspaper, or grab a quick bite to eat. The public sidewalks are like living rooms, and few living rooms would be livable without comfortable and attractive furniture.

So where is all the furniture on Seattle's streets? There are a few things scattered about. The seating along Fifth Avenue by Briazz Cafe and Tulio's Restaurant is terrific. The clutch of tables and chairs is one of the redeeming urban features of the otherwise suburban-looking Westlake Center. In good weather, a few espresso places set out tables. But not much else enlivens the sidewalk scene.

Sidewalks in other great cities are outfitted with fascinating features. Many of Portland's sidewalks are occupied with little food carts. Not in Seattle though; they are banned by our health department. In New York, you can scarcely walk more than a block without encountering a newsstand filled with a colorful display of newspapers and magazines. But not in Seattle.

Paris has its bouquinistes, the small purveyors of books, postcards, old magazines, and art along the Seine. Amsterdam, with a climate similar to ours, has magnificent sidewalk cafes that are used even in inclement weather because of parasol-like space heaters located between the seats. But not Seattle.

I know what you're thinking. "But what about all those espresso carts?" Yes, they're terrific and its wonderful that the city hasn't regulated them out of existence. (Although the rules are very specific about what can and cannot be sold.) But, as Peggy Lee once sang, "Is that all there is?"

About an hour's drive southwest of Paris, occupying a pastoral college campus-like setting, is a company with a very unusual mission: to make the sidewalks of the world's cities more convenient, attractive, and lively. The company—J.C. Decaux (pronounced like "deco")—hires well-known architects and industrial designers to develop types of outdoor "street furniture" specifically for pedestrians. They produce several lines of public restrooms, bus shelters, newspaper vending kiosks, benches, and directional signs.

Several years ago, the City of Seattle was approached by this firm with a proposal to install some of their handsome toilets and bus shelters. Their toilets are coin-operated, self-contained, and self-cleaning. Hundreds of these public loos have been in use in cities from Hamburg to Helsinki, from Lisbon to London. They have proven their reliability, cleanliness, and safety even in areas of heavy use. Decaux's designers have added a model that meets handicapped standards specifically for the American market.

The City of San Francisco bought the Decaux line of street furniture, including toilets, for Market Street. So well received have these been that more will be purchased for other locations. Similarly, New York City is reviewing proposals from Decaux and other companies such as Wall of Germany that offer similar products for public sidewalks.

These companies offer to build, install, and maintain these street furnishings at little or even no cost to local government. So how do they do it? By selling advertising space on the sides of some of the structures. The income from the panels is so lucrative that it more than pays for the installation and upkeep.

Now, you're probably thinking that you wouldn't care to see a barrage of cheesy ads for mouthwash and deodorant everywhere you walk. The ads placed by Decaux are hardly crass billboards. Because the cost of providing the kiosks and toilets is high, the advertising tends to be limited to high end products: internationally known perfumes, clothing, watches, jewelry, and the like. Graphic designers compose beautiful, often visually striking, images that are lighted at night, adding whimsy, warmth, and vitality to city streets.

So far, the City of Seattle has said "Thanks but no thanks." The city's Law

Department has said that local laws prohibit "off-premises" advertising. The city has restricted billboards, and in the eyes of the law, the proposed 4-by-6-foot signs would be just the same.

So here we have an irony. While the city seems to always be embattled in controversies over public restrooms in downtown, there are private companies that have already figured out how to do it and do it well.

I had suspected that, possibly, downtown property owners were the source of resistance. To the contrary, the Downtown Seattle Association has supported the idea. In fact, the roadblock seems to be that no one in City Hall is willing to be an advocate for changing the sign ordinance to allow these urban amenities to be provided. Sometimes, laws need to be examined to see if they are standing in the way more than helping.

17

Street Theater

I saw my first movie when I was six years old. It was called *Invaders From Mars,* and it was not my idea to see it. As a part of the birthday party for a kid in the neighborhood, his parents took us all out to see the movie. The film was terrifying. Its scenes of nasty, brain-drilling aliens and of people being sucked into the sand were so horrible that I held my hands tightly over my face for the entire two hours.

For the next week or so, I had nightmares so vivid that I can recall them to this day. But, despite the trauma, I grasped just how captivating and absorbing films could be. Since then, both movies and movie houses have held a particular fascination for me.

As a pre-driving teenager, I would study bus routes that would take me to one of the old, downtown movie palaces. Later, while in college, I would skip classes to take in a matinee. While living in New York for several years, I reveled in the highly charged atmosphere of people queuing up for opening nights. The combination of plush lobbies, bright lights, and crowds bustling about an ornately decorated ticket booth was, and still is, intoxicating.

Seattle is fortunate to have a host of movie theaters that are classy, intimate, and rich with character. Other cities have lost most of their charming theaters to development or to the phenomenon of suburban multiplexes. San Francisco, for all its sophistication, has virtually no older movie theaters left in its downtown or its close-in neighborhoods.

Seattle, on the other hand, has at least a dozen. The Harvard Exit and the Seven Gables are hard to beat for quaint, clubby ambiance. The Egyptian, with its richly decorated stage trim, is a splendid setting for enjoying films, even though its seats are inexcusably uncomfortable. The Uptown, the Neptune, the Guild, and the Varsity all engage the street, essentially treating the sidewalk as their lobby.

Seattle neighborhoods still retain many older,
charming movie theaters that engage the street.

It is this last aspect that distinguishes older movie theaters from their contemporary counterparts. The designers and builders of theaters knew that the entertainment began not with the credits but with the line out in front. People standing, strutting, posing, courting, cuddling, and creating a general buzz make the experience of seeing a movie that much richer. Great movies seduce us; great movie houses start the seduction at the sidewalk.

Some newer theaters demonstrate an understanding of the importance of the public realm. The Broadway Market Cinema faces a galleria packed with shops, cafes, vending carts, and people. The cinema complex in the US Bank Center is almost inseparable from the boisterous atmosphere of the open restaurant next door.

But too many new theaters suffer from being buried in the bowels of a larger building. The Newmark closed its doors, partly because it had no street presence. The Meridian 16 is barely better than a generic shopping mall multiplex. While the glass lobby is large, it has no sense of style or drama. The narrow electronic band of movie titles and show times is neither interesting nor readable. Give us a real movie marquee with bright lights, big letters, and a visible box office. Theaters, by their nature, need to be theatrical.

Other trends are also a bit distressing. I still miss the wonderfully eccentric little Pike Place Cinema with its entrance tucked into a recess along Post Alley.

Some of Seattle's quirky, homespun character used to come from the people staffing the independent theaters who stepped out before each film and introduced it with a bit of personal commentary.

The UA Cinemas on Sixth Avenue may not last much longer. Each day, the place seems to be running out of a few more letters for its marquee. A few years ago, the Music Hall was demolished, as were the Music Box, the Blue Mouse, and the grand old Orpheum many years before. The exterior of the Coliseum has been saved and reused for a clothing store, but as a theater it is gone.

Much of the liveliness of movie theater architecture was lost when movie attendance declined for a while in the '50s and '60s, and thousands of old theaters were boarded up or demolished. The federal government dealt a blow when it prohibited motion picture studios from owning theaters. The studios knew that the total experience of the movie-goer was important, not just what was up on the screen.

In recent decades, movies have enjoyed a huge resurgence in popularity, despite television and video. People intuitively know that many films are more enjoyable when shared with a lively audience than when viewed as a solitary activity. But what has not returned is a design that deepens the experience. Most contemporary movie theaters are the architectural equivalent of Tupperware—smooth, slick, and tightly sealed.

These places are impersonal, interchangeable containers designed principally for the sales of popcorn, soda pop, and the stuff that is sold from those columns of clear plastic tubing. At best, there is a smattering of neon and a few movie posters. What the builders and designers of newer theaters fail to comprehend is that theaters should be both engaging and elegant, sociable as well as sophisticated.

Perhaps we cannot return to lavishly appointed movie houses, but we can surely have something more than what appear to be lobbies of second-rate chain hotels. Recently, I got a small glimmer of hope when I came across a magnificent new movie house across from the Lloyd Center in Portland. There, a multiplex was placed right on the sidewalk and had a dramatic, domed rotunda. The individual theaters were arranged along a tall, interior galleria and each was marked by a distinctive and different marquee. There are some people who still understand movie theater architecture.

18

Remaking the
Urban Supermarket

One of the most standardized building types of the second half of the 20th century is the supermarket. Since the early 1950s, it seems as if every single structure made for the sale of groceries has been built from the same set of plans. The form is well-known to every school child in North America: a big box set back from the street, surrounded by a sea of parking, and set off by a billboard-sized sign. Only the name of the store is different.

This familiar formula has been duplicated in every community—historic to modern, from rural areas, to small towns, to suburbs, to city neighborhoods. In the location, orientation, and design of these stores, almost no thought has been given to the surrounding context. Sure, there might be a bit of brick pasted on the front or a fake dormer glued to the roof, but basically, these stores are architectural clones.

The result is that community after community has ended up with huge holes in its fabric. Older streets, which long held rows of contiguous storefronts, were blasted apart with expanses of asphalt that coated the landscape as well as the buildings within it. Newer cities never had much of chance to establish real, walkable neighborhoods. Supermarkets set up a pattern that then had to be followed by every other store. Suburbs even mandated this arrangement through their zoning laws.

Go into almost any city or town today and you see block after block of look-alike buildings with big false fronts of concrete block and a few windows behind treeless "front lawns" of blacktop. At night, the freeway-scale lighting fixtures hovering over the parking lots give them an eerie effect, much like an aircraft apron at an airport. So, while the big chain grocery stores brought food to communities, they did so by virtually tearing them apart.

Recently, however, cities have been demanding that these buildings show some respect. Ten years ago, Ralph's Market in San Diego became the centerpiece of a renovated and rebuilt neighborhood called Uptown. In downtown San Diego, Ralph's brick-faced store fills an entire block and offers a sidewalk cafe to passersby. In Vancouver, B.C.'s Fairview Heights neighborhood, the local Safeway store has most of its bulk and all of its parking underground. Only a small sign with the stylized "S" logo is visible from the street.

In Seattle, the Safeway in the Crown Hill neighborhood hugs the corner and has generous display windows along two streets. The parking is tucked discreetly to the side and is screened from surrounding homes. Too bad the store doesn't have individual outside doors to the various "boutiques" selling film, flowers, videos, and prepared food. Given that Safeway knocked down some long-standing small stores, putting a few shopfronts back on the sidewalk would have been the right thing to do.

This failing has been more than rectified by the new Harvard Market complex on Capitol Hill. The development contains a 45,000-square-foot QFC store, but the supermarket's size has been cleverly disguised by the bevy of independently operated, small shops that surround it. The developer, thankfully, did not force tenants to submit to a sign "theme." The resulting variety of awnings and signs, while not consistently well-designed, is suitably "messy" and urbane.

The really terrific aspect of Harvard Square is how it has healed a corner that for so long was a dismal parking lot. Shops now line the street. Two stories in height, the structure provides an appropriately scaled edge to the intersection. The facade of the building incorporates decorative terra cotta trim that had been on a building that was demolished. This is more than showing respect for a place, it is adding substantially to it.

The Harvard Market makes use of some of the details of a building that had occupied the site.

Mark Hinshaw

The QFC supermarket is burried within a complex of smaller shops and cafes.

Mark Hinshaw

Much of the parking is below ground, but some of it is on the roof. Because of the sloping site, the developer could create another set of shops on the second level, arranged around the parking. While the upper level resembles a strip mall, the parking is compact and the edges are defined by buildings, steel trellises, and the presence of old Fire Station 25 that was converted into condominiums 17 years ago.

The upper level of Harvard Market contains an open terrace overlooking the intersection of Broadway and East Pike Street. This is potentially a great addition to the neighborhood—if only the management would put out tables and chairs so that the space can actually be used. Too bad the architects missed an opportunity to create a whimsical pergola out of the elevator tower. This bland box looks like the custodian's closet. Perhaps a creative retrofit is forthcoming.

But, overall, this is fine piece of work. It fits the neighborhood. It creates a sense of place. It adds to the diversity of the city. Supermarkets need not dominate and subdue everything around them. Harvard Market shows that big stores can enhance the community as well as the bottom line.

CHAPTER

19

Good Books/Great Streets

A long-gone shop that I sorely miss in Seattle is one that was called the Silver Image. In both of its incarnations in Pioneer Square, it offered three things. It exhibited examples of fine photography—both classic and cutting edge. It had a fine selection of books, magazines, and monographs on the subject. And it thoroughly engaged the street.

Despite the loss of this particular store, we in Seattle are blessed with a set of choices that few cities can claim: a host of book shops specializing in all manner of subjects from the popular to the peculiar. While housing the written word, most of these purveyors add immeasurably to the life and liveliness of their surroundings.

Other big cities have examples of fusing publishing and public space. Along Boston's Newberry Street the odd little Spencer Mystery Books, wedged in among the narrow townhouses and cafes, sports a bay window that perfectly conveys its contents with a silhouetted figure of a man in a trench coat and fedora. The pencil thin Archivia bookstore on Madison Avenue in New York City is so chockablock with books on the arts that it is almost an extension of the Whitney Museum directly across the street.

The legendary Powell's in Portland, with its labyrinthine interior, places its coffee bar cum reading room right on the corner, in full view of passersby. Powell's has, arguably, spurred the renovation of an entire neighborhood—a district of art galleries, funky cafes, and lofts now affectionately known as The Pearl.

Like these books shops elsewhere, many of Seattle's counterparts have their own idiosyncratic personalities. However, all have a number of commonly held attributes. They signal their contents through visually appealing storefronts with generous expanses of glass that allow for people both inside and outside to see one another. They usually announce themselves with a careful-

Mark Hinshaw

The Cinema Books store is tucked into a corner of the building housing the Seven Gables Theater.

ly crafted sign that speaks to people on foot. They frequently have a slightly recessed entrance that gently draws you in. And, most important, they are part of a real, urban neighborhood, rather than a shopping mall.

Look at the diminutive Cinema Books up on Roosevelt Avenue near 50th Street. Tucked into the building housing the delightfully tatty Seven Gables Theater, this shop, with its simple neon sign, is an intriguing repository of cineastic literature. Although its previous location in Capitol Hill's Loveless Building was a perfect match, the current University District surrounding also works well.

Peter Miller Books on First Avenue appropriately echoes the design books it holds. A crisply tailored, modern storefront with sheets of glass framed by thin metal mullions is set within a richly detailed facade from the Art Deco era. When Peter holds a book-signing event, patrons spill out onto the sidewalk in a literal expression of street life. Few design book stores anywhere in this country are as entirely urbane.

Our own seller of mystery books, aptly named Mystery Books, is tucked into a cavernous, semi-underground space along Cherry Street. The great cast iron gate that frames the entrance is strongly suggestive of dark secrets and lies, murder and intrigue. Similarly, the Flora and Fauna bookstore occupies a subterranean space at First and Jackson. One can get a glimpse of the books by looking down into a light well. Slipping down into the store is like entering a cool grotto.

Left Bank Books actually looks as if it could incite a revolution, with strident titles that plaster the premises inside and out. Even the larger, general interest stores have their precious features. Elliott Bay Books is such an important landmark in Pioneer Square that I would fear for the neighborhood should it ever close. M. Coy Books on Pine Street is an elegant anchor for the revitalization of that downtown street.

Similarly, Bailey-Coy on Broadway, Madison Park Books, and Queen Anne Books all preside over neighborhoods that are vibrant and richly layered. Perhaps having a good bookstore is just as important to us as having a good coffee place.

But the grand prize winner for great Seattle bookstores, in my view, goes to the Wide World of Travel on 45th Street in Wallingford. This is a truly joyous place, filled with the promise of foreign lands, mysterious languages, and geography to be discovered. People are so happy to be in this store, anticipating trips to come. And the facade is magnificent, painted in exuberant colors. Flags flap gloriously in the breeze.

The display windows are filled with maps, guidebooks, and equipment essential for being immersed in other cultures. One can immediately enjoy a new purchase by gliding into the adjoining tea shop next door for a spot o' tea poured from a cozy-enshrouded pot. Usually packing the place are people sitting in quiet contemplation, poring over maps, or engaged in animated con-

The Wide World of Travel presents an exuberant facade to the street.

Mark Hinshaw

versations about past and future trips.

One of the curious aspects of book selling in Seattle is the absence of street vending, either by established stores or by independent purveyors. Most cities that are proud of their literary devotion, from London to Paris to New York, have numerous sidewalk locations at which to peruse and purchase new or used books. But not here.

You might be thinking, "The larger stores are probably preventing that." Or you might speculate, "The city probably requires exorbitant fees." You would be wrong. Seattle's laws do forbid virtually anything from being sold on the sidewalks other than flowers and coffee. But here's the mystery.

Courts have held that any restriction on the selling of books—even requiring permit fees—is an infringement on our most basic of freedoms, the First Amendment's protection of the freedom of speech. Yet no one here in this hotbed of in-your-face activism has dared try selling books from the sidewalk.

So here is an invitation, or perhaps a challenge. To established book merchants: Spill your guts. Line our sidewalks with your wares. To enterprising vendors: Set up carts and tables and temporary shelving. As Seattle has been becoming oh-so-trendy in the past few years, it has lost some of its soul. Here is a chance to get some of it back.

In the meantime, we have a whole panoply of fascinating book shops to patronize. Judging a book by its cover may be perilous. But assessing a bookstore by its architecture is marvelous.

IV

Urban Homes

ICON Architecture, LTD

One of the most startling recent changes in Citistate Seattle is the increasingly wide range of housing types. Not long ago many people scoffed at the notion that anyone would want to live in anything other than a single-family detached house. The real estate industry played to this sentiment, building larger and larger homes on larger and larger lots, further and further out into the countryside.

An annual "Street of Dreams" would feature obscenely bloated houses outfitted with luxurious features completely unaffordable for the majority of buyers. In this obsession with catering exclusively to upscale consumers, the industry all but ignored the growing number of singles, seniors, single-parent households, and young couples with modest incomes who did not want or could not afford what was being held up as the ideal.

Not anymore. We have realized that we cannot continue to expand outward, chewing up timberland and farmland without seriously damaging the natural environment that we value. Demographic changes might have caused an eventual redirection of the industry, but the state's Growth Management Act in 1990/1991 accelerated the process.

As a result, our selection of housing is much more varied. And the quality and character of housing has, on the whole, vastly improved. The following chapters describe examples of some of the new choices. In some cases, these choices are actually old. Builders have been discovering that we had a great tradition of smaller, simpler houses that still can meet the need of households today.

CHAPTER

20

Pitched Roofs
and Front Porches

Every July, a sand sculpture competition is held in Long Beach, Washington. Intricate and whimsical creations line up in a row along the beach. During the weekend, hundreds of people attempt to set the world's record for the longest continuous sculpture, made of sand.

On Sunday afternoon, the sculptures are overcome by the incoming tide. I cannot help but wish that we in the Seattle area could have some enormous wave come in and wipe out all of the monstrous housing developments that have been inflicted upon our neighborhoods during the past 15 years.

Of all of the metropolitan areas on the West Coast, we have built some of the worst examples of denser housing. Scores of apartment and condominium buildings have been cast across the urban landscape, with few displaying any sensibility toward building character or quality into our communities.

For the most part, they have been oversized, crudely fashioned behemoths that show little respect toward the context that surrounds them. Many are virtually interchangeable. What was built in Lynnwood was the same as in Greenwood, which was the same as in Lakewood.

Little wonder, then that neighborhood folks throughout the metropolitan area seem to immediately break out the petitions at the mere mention of a new project in their midst.

What we have is a vicious cycle. Neighborhoods fear the most egregious form of development: featureless, repetitive boxes, surrounded by aprons of asphalt. And that is precisely what they seem to get, thereby reinforcing the notion that anything other than single-family housing is second class and suspect.

Architects Michael Pyatok & Associates created an elegant, dignified home for transitional families.

The great tragedy in this is that never before have we needed more choices in housing. The American ideal of the large house on the large lot is affordable to only a minority of the households in this region. What's more, the fastest growing segments of the population are singles, single-parent households, and seniors—most of whom could do just fine in a row house, cottage house, accessory dwelling, or a small house on a small lot.

We may decry the "decline" of the traditional family unit, but it is simply happening. As a metropolitan region, we have to start welcoming ways of accommodating new and different households. And most of these households, despite the popular myth that hordes of newcomers are crossing our borders daily, will be composed of people, or the children of people, who already live here. They are our kids, our parents, our friends. "They" are us.

Unfortunately, most local zoning codes forbid anything other than conventional single-family detached houses or apartments. But, it is precisely the smaller, more compact and modest types of housing that have, throughout the story of this country, allowed individuals and families with limited incomes access to the housing market. Although some communities are beginning to loosen up their restrictive laws, we have a long way to go before alternatives will be widely available.

What's more, relatively few architects and even fewer builders seem to be able to produce housing in higher density forms that both provide a gracious place in which to live and fit comfortably into a neighborhood. Although it is not easy to find many positive examples, there are a handful throughout the region.

Out in Issaquah, the master-planned community of Klahanie demonstrates that some architects and builders can provide decent, sensitively designed housing that is denser than the typical subdivision but exhibits qualities that we associate with single-family homes. Oxford Park consists of townhouse-like condominiums grouped around two grassy hillocks. The buildings incorporate peaked roof forms, small scale proportioning, and traditional wood detailing. The effect is one of a small village, rather than a "complex."

In Redmond, the YWCA commissioned a transitional housing development for homeless and displaced families, called the "Family Village." The building has a broad overhanging pitched roof, a rich combination of materials, and well-detailed trim. Suggesting a sense of "home," it demonstrates that housing that is often thought of as institutional can be given real dignity.

In Bellevue, several blocks east of that city's downtown, Park Highland is a sizable development. But it has been broken up into groupings that have different, but related, design features. The common community building has small apartments on the second floor. Most of the parking has been placed underneath the buildings, leaving much more area for landscaped spaces. The design reflects a solid tradition of wood frame, craftsman-style housing that has been a hallmark of this region.

In Seattle, Ballard Square condominiums presents the neighborhood with a development that is classy and urbane. Following wave after wave of dreary, flat-topped boxes fitted out with repetitive balconies, Ballard now offers a positive role model. The building uses color creatively to reduce the apparent bulk of the building. A handsome brick wall defines the sense of entry and private spaces around it. The combination of horizontal banding, bay windows, and visible chimneys gives the appearance that this is a collection of individual homes, not merely "units."

Cascade Court apartments, at the corner of Seneca and Summit in Seattle's First Hill neighborhood, is a superb example of expertly designed urban hous-

Yannis Paris

Cascade Court, designed by GGLO Architects, subtly echoes the adjacent historic mansion.

The quality of details and materials used in Cascade Court gives no clue that it is low-income housing.

ing. Built for low- and moderate-income families, it is nonetheless as distinguished and sophisticated as any market rate housing. This is a development that clearly respects the setting. The height and massing on the south side fit comfortably next to the venerable Stimson Green Mansion. A masonry chimney on the new structure subtly echoes the chimney on the mansion. The interior courtyard, glimpsed from the street through an entry portal, contains a play structure. Projecting window bays are supported by oversized wooden brackets, an unexpected but delightful touch. Portions of the project are topped with fanciful peaked "caps."

All of these exemplary developments share a number of simple design principles. The bulk of each building is broken into small increments. Pitched roofs are used, often in a gabled form. Some semblance of a front porch is frequently found. And delicate, humane touches like horizontal trim boards, brackets, and wide window casing are used.

All this is done without being self-consciously "cute." These buildings draw upon a long tradition in this region of solid, well-crafted, wood frame housing. Most importantly, they prove that higher density housing can be a good neighbor.

Ask any child in North America to draw a picture of a house. Almost assuredly, it will have a peaked roof, a chimney, generous windows, and a prominent front door. From a very early age, we all know the things that symbolize "home." There is no huge mystery here. But what is truly a mystery is why so many builders, and even many designers, just don't seem to get it.

21

Housing That Fits

Until recently, there were few examples in Seattle of higher density residential development designed to fit sensitively into its surroundings For example, a recent development up on Lake City Way turns a five-story blank wall toward the street, offering a rude landmark to that already bleak stretch of road.

Downtown Seattle has had its own share of dreadful residential developments. The featureless building wedged into an odd-shaped site along Elliott Avenue near the Alaskan Way viaduct is hardly mitigated by the addition of a silly green awning along the parapet. And the propriety of plucking a kitschy tower from Honolulu and plunking it down within a stone's throw of the Pike Place Market surely should have been questioned by someone.

But despite these egregious examples, there is a counter trend, one that suggests we might be finally on the way to seeing housing that respects its neighborhood and offers choices that have not been, until recently, available.

Mark Hinshaw

Fremont Court mixes apartments with street level commercial uses.

Several years ago, Kauri Investments built a splendid project on Fremont Avenue North, just south of N.E. 45th. The building provides 25 moderately priced apartments surrounding a courtyard that is recessed from the street. Ground level shops animate the street. Fremont Court incorporates a cascading roof, horizontal wood siding, and window details that echo the older housing in the vicinity.

Jim Potter is proud of his company's knack for providing pleasant places for people to live while, at the same time, being careful about keeping costs down. The trick is in the proportioning, the landscaping, and the finishing touches— all items that many builders seem to care little about.

On Capitol Hill, the nonprofit Housing Resources Group of Seattle developed Mercer Court at the corner of Mercer and 12th Avenue. The architects borrowed from forms found elsewhere in the neighborhood and created a building that looks as if it has been there for decades. Developed for low- and moderate-income households, the place resembles an upscale condominium. A pleasant garden at the corner gives a splash of seasonal color to the intersection.

Mercer Court offers evidence that even projects with tight budgets can be gracious. Far too many developers use cost constraints as an excuse for austerity when hiring a thoughtful architect could make all the difference. Contrary to popular myth, good design need not cost more.

Mercer Court looks like it has been a part of the neighborhood for decades.

That good design can make a difference is also demonstrated by a fine development called El Patio on Beacon Hill. El Patio surrounds an interior courtyard that offers play space for children who live there. Kitchens and dining rooms overlook the space, offering observation of outside activities.

Finally, a number of nonprofit organizations throughout the city are sponsoring the construction of low-cost homes. Built by a combination of volunteer labor and the "sweat equity" of the future homeowner, some of these houses hearken back to the era when builders offered simple but attractive structures for people with modest incomes. In recent decades, most single-family housing developers have catered to people who want an ostentatious display of wealth: a house attached to a three-car garage.

Though it has previously concentrated on building individual houses, Habitat for Humanity recently built a project that consists of townhouses, a building type that used to be seen in Seattle, though not in recent decades. Located in the Central Area, it consists of a row of three buildings arranged around a shared courtyard. The design fits nicely with nearby single-family residences.

None of these projects would likely be awarded prizes for high-style design. But all demonstrate a principle that is more important than advancing the cutting edge of architecture. New, more diverse forms of housing must be provided to broaden our choices and enliven our neighborhoods.

22

Loft Living

Artists Karen Guzak and Warner Blake live and work in an eccentrically furnished loft in the Sunny Arms Co-op, a building designed as an adaptive reuse by architect Patricia Brennan.

In the early 1970s, the first artists were beginning to occupy a bunch of abandoned warehouse buildings in New York City. The area, wedged between Houston Street and Canal Street, Little Italy and the Hudson River, was still home to numerous factories, distributing companies, and fabricators.

Most of the buildings had been constructed in an era when multistory operations were the norm. By the 1970s, many of the structures were unused and decrepit. Though it was not, strictly speaking, legal for artists to live in buildings zoned for industrial use, the city turned a blind eye. All except the fire department. Any building with an artist living in it had to have a plaque containing the letters A.I.R.—"artist in residence"—so that firefighters would be alerted to the presence of a person.

Two decades later, what is now widely known as SoHo has spawned many similar live/work districts. Baltimore, Chicago, Oakland, Portland, Vancouver, Denver, and others have seen their older industrial districts transformed into lively places filled with galleries, cafes, and coffeehouses. San Francisco's South of Market district is so expansive and energetic it has spawned an entire subculture in that city.

Here in Seattle, we have not seen any distinct district emerge, although portions of Belltown, Georgetown, and the Pike/Pine corridors have many of the same characteristics as these areas in other cities. During the past six years we have seen the adaptive reuse and development of several unusual buildings specifically aimed at people in the arts.

Back in 1989, a former shoe factory on the edge of Georgetown was converted into the Sunny Arms Artists Cooperative. A pioneering effort by artist/developer Karen Guzak, the building demonstrated that there was a market for roughly finished spaces. Today it is filled with painters, sculptors, glass blowers, and performance artists. Some of the larger units are ideal for occasional soirees, in which musicians and actors present pieces to small audiences of colleagues.

Previously, the APEX Cooperative in Belltown had offered simple, low-cost spaces for artists who desired to live downtown, despite the rapidly rising cost of real estate. In the APEX, economies were gained by using a common kitchen and dining area. But the Sunny Arms was the first time that a full-scale, loft-style structure was renovated for artists' habitation.

These two initial forays into an uncommon form of housing were not immediately followed by other similar efforts. But over the past several years, a number of projects have been completed, suggesting that the concept has finally caught on.

In 1993, the Union Art Co-op opened on East Union Street in a building that had originally held a automobile dealership. The industrial facade is intact while the internal space offers live/work apartments of various sizes. A pleasant garden crowns the rooftop. Within the galleries on the ground floor, both well-established and newly emerging artists show their work.

In 1994, the Seattle Chapter of the American Institute of Architects broke a tradition of recognizing single-family homes in its Home of the Month program by selecting the Union Art Co-op as an exemplary, albeit atypical, piece of residential architecture. We need to reward developments demonstrating that single-family detached dwellings are not the only acceptable option.

In recent years, the Banner Building at Western Avenue and Vine Street has amassed a growing list of kudos. The American Institute of Architects—at the local, the regional, and the national levels—has praised this new building for its innovative approach to mixing living and working environments as well as units aimed at widely varying incomes.

The Banner Building was a labor of love for its originator, Koryn Rolstad. Rolstad, who owns the ground floor fabrication company that gave the building its name, threw herself at the project for several years with relentless but exhausting zeal. Her vision of having a high-profile, high-style place in the midst of downtown gave rise to a distinctive and elegant landmark. Unfortunately, the current owners are marketing the units not just to artists, as originally intended, but to anyone with sufficient cash.

Michael Jensen

Architect Patricia Brennan designed this conversion of an industrial building into a live/work cooperative for artists.

Nevertheless, the Banner Building retains an exquisite, bare bones esthetic that unabashedly expresses its muscular construction. The Spartan concrete frame has been fitted with floor-to-ceiling windows, angular metal balconies, and landscaped terraces. The lower, hump-backed building along the alley contains small, low-income units.

Seeing workers scurry about inside Rolstad's storefront along Western is a bit of free street theater. Indeed, the initial idea was to fill these deep spaces with active fabrication companies. Too bad an antique store was placed on the corner rather than the cafe that was originally intended. Static displays of objects do not offer the same degree of animation as actual people.

Across the street to the south is a building that goes only by its address—81 Vine. This rather ordinary old brick building was renovated several years ago. It now has a sense of style and sophistication far different from its humble origins as a paper box company.

81 Vine, like its predecessors, is filled with a lively mixture of people in the arts: artists, musicians, architects, landscape designers, event producers, photographers, and the like. The building shares an intimate little courtyard with the low-income apartment building to its south. A fine new cafe graces the corner. Architect Carolyn Geiss, the designer and co-owner of the building, has also contributed to the growing sense of community in the north end of the Regrade by being involved in developing the Belltown P-patch nearby, as well as advocating street improvements.

All of these buildings required extraordinary feats of dedication and perseverance by their proponents. They had to deal with a nightmarish array of hurdles thrown in their path by bankers, building codes, and construction costs.

Architects Weinstein/Copeland designed this new live/work building with simple industrial forms and materials.

Ironically, such efforts can go awry without special legal devices such as cooperative ownership that help ensure that artists are the preferred occupants. As has happened in SoHo, loft buildings, with their "cool" spare image, are becoming high-priced commodities. Eventually, artists are shoved aside by stockbrokers and attorneys who want the aesthetic but not the culture that goes along with it.

But for now, these buildings offer local artists an opportunity to have spaces to live and work right in the heart of the city, contributing immensely to its diversity and its vitality.

23

Winslow Builds Housing the Right Way

Over the last few years, some of the most interesting and unusual housing in the region has been built in Winslow, on the west side of Elliott Bay. Though now designated as the town center of the recently incorporated City of Bainbridge Island, Winslow still retains its individual small town character. This is a place where folks smile at strangers and say hello. Shopkeepers and cafe owners chat up customers. And neighbors are bound to run into one another at the Town and Country store.

It is perhaps not surprising that Winslow should have so many fine examples of new and innovative residential development. Many of the best architects and landscape architects in the region work there or live there. The place also has an unusually large number of enlightened property owners and developers.

The Winslow Co-housing development has received national attention for its combination of design excellence and participatory planning. The architect worked along with the homeowners in laying out the configuration and design of units. The result is an intimate, village-like collection of houses, apartments, common buildings, and green space. Though this co-housing project has received much attention from the professional and popular media, there are a number of other projects which, while less well known, are also commendable.

At the corner of Winslow Way and Madison Avenue is Winslow Green. Built in the mid-'80s, it consists of two floors of condominiums that sit atop a row of shops and cafes. Display windows sparkle with merchandise while locals lounge on the plaza and sip coffee. The development wraps around a rectangular expanse of grass that has served as a sort of village green. This is a superb

Architect Greg Hackworth designed the Madison Cottages in Winslow. He borrowed from the traditions associated with small, turn-of-the century homes.

Greg Hackworth

example of mixed use. While it probably wouldn't win any awards for superior design or craftsmanship, it feels just right.

Up Madison, at the corner of Wyatt Street, sits a development that is appropriately named Wyatt's Corner. This is an unusual example of mixing residential and retail uses together. The main structure is a sophisticated saltbox that contains an elegant retail store on the ground floor. Above it are three dwellings that share a planted terrace.

To the south of this building is a clutch of structures that look as if they might be a different development. But they are not. Three narrow row houses have tiny front and rear gardens. Behind them is a garage with a carriage house perched on top. These houses point out how useless and wasteful are the big front lawns that are the hallmark of so many residential developments.

The Madison Cottages have rear alleys that are used by residents for socializing.

Each cottage is approximately 1,200 square feet and is slightly different from its neighbors.

Further north on Madison is a cluster of semi-attached homes that are tucked in behind what at first appears to be a simple, contemporary house. These dwellings are sociable as well as private. They are designed to minimize the repetition typically associated with attached units. Tiny porches allow residents to sit outside.

Directly across the street is the newly completed Madison Cottages. These small, tightly spaced houses echo the proportions and details found in simple, wood frame houses built in the early years of this century. Each is slightly different from one another. But they have all have front porches and pitched roofs. One-car garages are tucked neatly off narrow alleys. So successful has this project been that a second phase of houses immediately followed.

What all of these developments demonstrate is that there are many forms of housing other than the two we have been getting in recent decades: sprawling subdivisions or cookie-cutter apartments. These projects are denser than typical single-family housing, but not dense in a way that frightens some folks. And they have a considerable amount of style.

Higher density need not be dreaded. It is how it is designed and arranged on a site that makes the difference. In fact, it can be argued that projects such as these use land more responsibly, preserve existing vegetation, and make more efficient use of energy and materials than the standard forms of residential development. They also help build a sense of community that respects the past and fits the nature of our region far better than what is typically available on the market today.

Despite the surveys that tell us that people prefer to own a large, single-family home on a large lot, most new households can no longer afford it. The challenge is to design and build places to live that offer a blend of privacy, community, affordability, and style.

24

Small Houses on Small Lots

Over the past couple of decades, one of the most persistent and pervasive myths is that the cost of labor and materials have made houses increasingly expensive to build. Nothing could be further from the truth.

In fact, the home building industry has been extraordinarily creative in coming up with less costly forms of construction, using synthetic products, "engineered wood," and labor-saving techniques. On a cost-per-square foot basis, building costs have remained stable and, compared with inflation, decreased somewhat. The effect of these improvements has mostly been canceled out by other factors.

So what has made the cost of housing go up over the years? There are two principal causes. One is simply that houses have gotten bigger. Studies of house sizes over the years have shown a marked increase from an average of less than 1,500 square feet to more than 2,000 square feet today. Every additional square foot has added to the eventual price to consumers.

Another major reason is the cost of land. In most communities—especially those in the Puget Sound region that is laced with streams and wetlands and surrounded by steep slopes and mountains—buildable land is a commodity in short supply. In a classic case of textbook economics, if the supply of any product is constrained and demand increases, the price goes up. What has exacerbated the limitation on supply is our collective obsession with unnecessarily large lots.

For most of the history of this country, families—sometimes large families—lived in relatively small houses on relatively small lots anywhere from 3,000 to 5,000 square feet. No one suffered. Kids grew up, found places to play, explored their neighborhoods, all without having huge backyards. Many of us who were born during the middle part of this century can recall a childhood in a little two- or three-bedroom house wedged onto a small parcel of property.

The not-for-profit housing developer HomeSight built these small houses with designs that echo older urban homes.

Mark Hinshaw

ICON Architects designed these small, but visually complex dwellings to serve lower-income families.

Courtesy of ICON Architecture

It's not even necessary to rely upon memory; many cities and towns still have perfectly wonderful pre-World War II neighborhoods filled with modest homes on relatively small lots.

The problem is, in many communities, lots of this size are simply not legal. Sometime in the years following the war, local governments decided that lots of 7,000 to 8,000 square feet were the minimum necessary. No matter that not a single shred of evidence in sociology or behavioral science supported this. Nevertheless, in cities throughout the country, laws governing the parcelization of land were passed that wiped an entire type of housing completely off the books.

For over 200 years, small "starter" homes offered young households the opportunity to own property, and to maintain and expand their own dwelling. It also enabled families to gradually progress through the housing market by trading up. But in matter of few decades, that possibility was all but eliminated. And we now scratch our heads and agonize over the decrease in affordable housing.

But things are changing. Gradually some communities are realizing that the solution is in their own hands. They are again allowing developers to create small houses in compact arrangements. These are aimed precisely at segments of the market that are expanding the most: seniors, singles, single-parent households, and young, middle-income couples. Previously, these households had little choice but to rent an apartment or purchase a condominium.

Up in Lynden, near the Canadian border, Greenfield Village looks much like a neighborhood that might have been built at the turn of the last century. Modest, simplified Victorian homes with front porches sit closely together on narrow streets. Garages are accessible from a rear alley. The neighborhood includes a small park and the streets are as serene as any suburban subdivision. No two houses look exactly alike, although there is a resemblance that holds the buildings together as a whole—precisely the method that builders of smaller homes used to use to create many fine residential districts.

The developer built these terrific little gems by following a "pattern book" of houses that was published about a hundred years ago. Greenfield Village has been so well received in the marketplace that the company is building more of these "new-traditional" neighborhoods in Ferndale, Burlington, and Oak Harbor.

In Black Diamond, the house designs in Diamond Village recall some of the best features found in older urban neighborhoods like Montlake, Wallingford, and Ballard in Seattle. If one element is lacking, it is trees; the developer would have been wise to sprinkle the development with a few large trees.

Perhaps the most intriguing of these new, but old, developments are the homes that have been developed by HomeSight here in Seattle. At the corner of 24th Avenue E. and Yesler is a full-block collection of finely crafted small houses. Again, each is a bit different in design, but there are similar details and materials. These homes have individual garages that are located off short rear alleys.

HomeSight developed another cluster of homes with a similar design along Martin Luther King Way, just north of the park over Interstate 90. In the range of 900 to 1,400 square feet, the houses are selling for $100,000 to $137,000. Developments such as these prove that houses can be modest in both size and price, fit within a neighborhood, and exhibit a sense of style.

The HomeSight development, fortunately, is platted to allow homeowners to own the plot of property on which their house sits. Not so with many others. Far too many jurisdictions still do not allow small lots as a matter of right. Small houses must, therefore, sit on land owned in common. Even so, this often requires a special approval that involves unnecessary time and expense. There is absolutely no reason why small lot development cannot simply be allowed.

What a pity that local governments wring their hands about affordable housing and then frustrate the very attempts to provide it. The mechanism that helped create thousands of safe, compact, and livable neighborhoods all across the country has been virtually forbidden by law. It is high time to return to this fine, traditional way of building great towns and cities.

25

Tucked-Away Town Homes

Throughout North America, many cities have already found ways to accommodate urban density that create fine, livable neighborhoods. For example, Boston's Back Bay is filled with delightful brownstones hugging tree-lined streets. San Francisco's row house neighborhoods are fabled for their gracious ambiance. Denver's Cherry Creek district has seen sensitively designed infill developments that build upon the established character.

Up in Vancouver, B.C., the city established a special form of land-use regulation for the Kitsilano neighborhood. Owners of older, larger homes can receive permits to convert the structures into two units if they bring the buildings up to code and restore them to their former splendor. The door to the second unit must be discreetly located so as not to change the single-family appearance. In return, the owner may build two more small units in the back yard, accessible from the alley.

Because parking must be provided on-site, owners must be very clever in the arrangement of new and existing buildings. The city staff reviews designs to ensure that new construction matches the architectural character of the existing buildings and that new windows do not overlook someone else's home or backyard. The result is astonishing. The street scene is unchanged—stately single-family structures with well-landscaped front yards. But, the density is actually 30 dwelling units per acre, an amount we typically associate with boxy apartment buildings.

Seattle has been slow to explore such innovative approaches. Neighborhoods have often resisted anything that is different. But perhaps they are not entirely off-base. In recent decades, builders have kept to standardized forms that were insensitive to community character. The city, for its part, tried—with a stunning lack of success—to regulate design through mathematical formulas.

But throughout Seattle, there is evidence that people are being creative in

Mark Hinshaw

This rear-lot accessory dwelling fits comfortably with the main house and surrounding neighborhood.

opening up more options for people who do not want or who cannot afford a single-family detached house. Some folks have discovered a neat trick: borrowing from the past. This city, like most others, had a well-developed tradition of providing many options for living modestly. After all, most households have been middle class and could never purchase a big house. It is only in the past few decades that we have, as a country, held up the large detached house as an ideal.

The Eastlake neighborhood is sprinkled with widely varying and fascinating attempts at carefully inserting different housing types to meet a range of needs. Young couples, singles, seniors, students, and families with kids all have many choices. The best part is that the density is sufficiently great to support neighborhood services, shops, and cafes, as well as frequent transit. If you miss a bus, it's probably not 10 minutes until the next one rolls up.

The neighborhood contains several forms of housing that have not been built in recent years, but could serve other parts of the region very well. The simple, brick row houses on Roanoke are small but dignified. On Minor Avenue E., south of Lynn Street, a cluster of four modest, wood frame houses shares a common driveway and internal parking court. A block away on Yale Avenue E., a Victorian–era structure has a storybook-like cottage of a more recent vintage at its rear.

One of the most creative recent projects is a house on Minor Avenue E. just north of Boston. From the street, this new home looks like it could have been built around the turn of the century. A generous porch frames the door to the main floor, which is elevated several feet above the ground—a classic way of providing privacy for the residents as well as "eyes on the street." Lap siding is used on the lower floor with shingles on the upper floor, offering a richly layered effect.

Vertically proportioned windows framed with wide wood trim are divided into small panes (not the fake, prefab kind), reinforcing the traditional look. Large wood brackets supporting the roof overhang and an arbor offer a degree of drama. As an example of urban infill, the proportioning and detailing are extraordinarily well done.

But, a real surprise is to be found in the rear, invisible from the street. Along the alley, there is a small cottage, set above the garage. This is hardly a meager apartment. It has a generous deck and a distinctive roof line that gives it a cozy look. Although it shares the lot with the larger, newer house, none of its windows look directly into the back yard. Nor does the nicely detailed rear porch on the main house intrude into the privacy of the cottage. Such a careful respect for people's personal space is so often lacking in new development.

The result is two splendid homes on one lot, set along a pleasant street. Each dwelling can appeal to a different type of household. And it did not take a big development company to do it. It was accomplished in the best tradition of home-grown, small-scale entrepreneurial energy—people rebuilding their own neighborhoods.

This kind of creativity and sensitivity is exactly what Seattle and other cities need to encourage. We must reexamine all of our policies, codes, and procedures to embrace and reward these efforts. The solutions to our housing dilemma have always been with us. We need merely to rediscover them.

26

Return of the Row House

We are the only country that divides our choices of housing into two separate categories: single family and multiple family. What the rest of the world has long known, but what we have seemingly not grasped, is that there are many, many different types of houses. Cottage homes, courtyard houses, carriage houses, flats, maisonettes, tandem houses, attached houses, and detached houses, to name just a few.

What we have set up for ourselves with this simplistic notion is nothing less than a cruel hoax: If you cannot afford to own a large home on a large lot, you are somehow second class. Now this is a terrible social tragedy—and one that is getting progressively worse. Fewer and fewer people can actually afford what has been held up as the American dream. What's more, fewer and fewer people need it.

Over the past several years, many people purchasing homes in the metropolitan area have been discovering a housing form that had all but disappeared for a number of decades: the row house.

Now, the Seattle area never had a tradition of entire neighborhoods filled with row houses like San Francisco and Baltimore. But Seattle had them. It is possible to still find little pockets in many older parts of Seattle, Everett, and Tacoma. Some were developed before the turn of the century. Many more from that era either burned down or were torn down before preservation forces prevailed. John Chaney of Historic Seattle notes that row houses were found in many close-in neighborhoods like Denny Hill and First Hill, but were demolished during massive regrading projects.

Row houses were built even into the 1920s. The Tudor–style brick row at Eastlake and Roanoke is an example. But after the Depression, row houses were rarely built.

In the decades following World War II, cities began to adopt minimum lot

Gary Sutto

The LionsGate development by GGLO Architects mixes row houses with street-level commercial space.

sizes. Typically these were set at 6,000 to 7,000 square feet—several times greater than that needed for a row house. In the span of one generation, we almost completely wiped out a type of housing that had served us well for 200 years.

There was a brief revival in the 1970s throughout the Seattle area. The group of attached houses at 10th Avenue and Highland are still exceptionally elegant and sophisticated. The several groupings of row houses laced through portions of Madison Park are not as refined in the quality of construction, but have matured rather well nonetheless.

Trouble was, some of what was tried back then was often awkwardly arranged, cramped, and had poor sound insulation in the common walls. What's more, they were often designed repetitively, with little variety and with little recognition of their context. Consequently, neighbors protested, the city caved in, and ordinances allowing them were repealed.

But things change. Today, households are much more diverse in age, character, and composition. Families are smaller. People are aging; the kids have grown up and left home. Singles and young couples are hard pressed to get into the conventional, single-family detached housing market.

Row houses are, in fact, single-family homes, except that they are attached to their neighbors, rather than detached from them. They offer the same attributes with respect to ownership, responsibility, privacy, and personalization. They can be simple and affordable, or they can be elaborate and expensive.

Row houses are ideal for urban neighborhoods, in that density can be accommodated without radically changing character. Carefully designed row houses can look like they are separate, even though they are not. They use land more responsibly, not wasting space for side yards. They use energy more efficiently, with fewer exterior walls. And they fall into the range of density for which frequent transit service can be cost-effectively provided.

Over the past several decades, the building industry has given us essentially only two choices: individual houses on large lots at densities that are generally less than seven dwellings per acre, or apartments that are more than 20 dwelling units per acre. Row houses are generally built at around 10 to 15 units per acre—a range of density that has been sorely missing in our communities.

Recently, there have been a number of new developments that have reintroduced row houses into the regional marketplace. This time around, the places are well designed, well built, and sometimes even quite elegant.

Down in Dupont, in the new community of Northwest Landing, there is a small clutch of row houses called "Bay Colony" that face a village green. They are arranged and designed in a neotraditional manner, drawing upon Craftsman-style elements found in the original town of Dupont next door. Other homes in Northwest Landing, while not actual row houses, are small and traditional in design.

LionsGate row houses on the main street contain a small commercial space accessible both from the sidewalk and directly from the dwelling.

Eduardo Calderon

There is additional evidence that row houses are returning. One row house development in Seattle, on Fairview Avenue East and Boston Street, sold out within a few weeks. The dwellings are compact and nicely proportioned, with single-car garages, stoops, balconies, and small rear yards. Any neighborhood should surely be pleased to have these in their midst.

Another in the Phinney Ridge neighborhood features roof lines, window trim, and colors echoing those of other, older houses found in that neighborhoods. In Bellevue, One Central Park on Richards Road sold like hotcakes. These spacious, vertically oriented homes have fine wood detailing throughout and cozy, sunlit rooms. The stepped interior layout offers unusually high ceilings that give an illusion of spaciousness.

Perhaps the most innovative and forward-thinking example of row houses in this region is a development called LionsGate in downtown Redmond. These row houses appeal to people who want to work at home *and* have a distinct place of business. Houses that front on the main street include small commercial spaces accessible from the sidewalk. There are several larger spaces for convenience stores and corner cafes.

The entire development resembles a compact village arranged around narrow streets and squares. The best thing about this kind of development is that it is happening exactly where it should. It is within a short walk of the city center, the library, parks, public buildings, and transit. It is convenient, comfortable, and attractive. It looks and feels like a real urban neighborhood.

The row house is definitely back. We should welcome the return of a housing type that is both refreshingly new and one of our best urban traditions.

PART

V

Public Spaces/Sacred Places

The recently opened Benaroya Hall for the Seattle Symphony offers a restful plaza in the middle of downtown Seattle.

The mark of any great city is the number, variety, and quality of places that its residents feel impassioned about. Vitally important to urban life, they contribute to what is meant when people say they value "community."

Back in the late '60s and early '70s, Seattle—like cities elsewhere—began to see its history destroyed. Pioneer Square, the original town center, was dismissed as just so many scruffy old buildings. Pike Place Market was seen as

109

standing in the way of more lucrative downtown development. Farmlands were rapidly being replaced by warehouses and strip malls.

Several watershed events took place during this era that fundamentally altered the course of the city and the region. Pioneer Square and the Pike Place Market were saved from the wrecking ball. The city set up public commissions to oversee public art, the preservation of historic buildings, and the design of civic structures and spaces. At the same time, the state adopted an Environmental Policy Act, which mandated that impacts both public and private be identified. The Shorelines Management Act protected beaches, rivers, streams, and wetlands. In less than a decade, these efforts were paying off.

People in Citistate Seattle now assume that these aspects of the region are being cared for. Beyond that, we are now seeing a wholly new phenomenon: New places are being created that instill strong attachments. Huge new parks have been provided, some without programmed recreational facilities. Many people value the simple quietude and restorative qualities of green space. Most of the region's historic buildings have been completely restored, many given new life with unusual combinations of uses.

The cumulative result is a collective respect for parts of our past and elements of our natural environment. These spaces and places temper the form of new development and create a rich layering of experiences and memories.

27

Preserving the Past

Thirty years ago I watched a city rip its own heart out. The political and business leaders of Oklahoma City had become enamored with a new plan that promised to transform that midwestern city into a showcase of gleaming glass towers, shopping arcades, sunken gardens, and soaring sky bridges. Put together by one of the nation's leading architects, the plan called for leveling virtually all of the downtown and starting over again.

The city set up an urban renewal authority which, over the subsequent decade, pushed over, tore down, or blew up dozens of older buildings. A few of these were memorialized on film as they imploded. The clips are often shown in movies when some director wants to represent an urban disaster.

Within a few years, wonderful old streets simply disappeared. Reno Street, which was lined for blocks with second hand stores, was gutted. Elsewhere, entire blocks were cleared of structures containing hotels, offices, shops, and apartments. Many of these older buildings had been built in the early decades of the 20th century and were architectural gems.

The tragedy is that after all the destruction was finished, little got built, save for a gargantuan and extraordinarily ugly convention center, a performing arts theater that is now abandoned and surrounded by weeds, a bizarre, cylindrical glass structure containing plants, and a handful of other mediocre projects. Downtown Oklahoma City is now virtually lifeless—a place without a soul.

As Oklahoma City was busy destroying its history, Seattle was taking steps to save its older buildings and districts. Pioneer Square, Pike Place Market, old Ballard, Columbia City, and many other areas and individual structures throughout the city were preserved and rehabilitated. The fact that we have these pieces of our heritage is due to the heroic efforts of hundreds of dedicated people and a number of special-purpose organizations.

One of these organizations is the Historic Seattle Preservation and

Architects Boyle/Wagoner remodeled this former home for needy women into a spectacular community center.

Development Authority. Formed in 1974, it is the only nonprofit organization that operates on a citywide basis to preserve historic structures and landscapes. Historic Seattle has been responsible for renovating dozens of buildings, giving them new uses and a continued role to play in the community.

Al Elliott served as Historic Seattle's executive director during its initial 14 years. "Historic Seattle was a unique entity," says Elliott. "It was set up by the city expressly to allow the purchase and preservation of valuable buildings that might otherwise have been destroyed." The authority was empowered to issue tax-free bonds to provide financing, but could also act much like a private developer—a role that constitutional law denies cities in this state.

Several projects exemplify the unique contribution of Historic Seattle to the fabric of the community. One is a commercial building, one is institutional, the other is residential. They demonstrate the breadth and complexity of accomplishments by this important organization.

The Mutual Life Building is located on one of the prime intersections in Pioneer Square: First and Yesler. The building was one of many originally designed by architect Elmer Fisher after the great fire in 1889 had leveled most of the original town center. In 1982, after decades of substantial deterioration, Historic Seattle obtained title and secured financing. The building was carefully restored.

At the corner, a toy store occupies both the street level and the level below the street. The lower level is reached by a set of exterior stairs that were rediscovered during the process of renovation. The store's cavernous, vaulted interior, with sandstone walls and columns, provides a glimpse of the structural solidity and classic proportioning of this Victorian–Romanesque style building.

The handsome, soaring arch along First Avenue is both muscular and refined. Nocturnal street musicians frequently use the arched recess as an enormous megaphone. The renovation work restored the glass skylights that were used to bring daylight down into the areaways below the sidewalk, an element that is important to the history of Pioneer Square.

Inside, the lobby and elevator contain fine details and fittings. Though somewhat small, they are sufficiently elegant to make an instant impression on visitors. Walking into the First Mutual Building makes the experience of entering most contemporary buildings pale by comparison.

Designed by C. Alfred Breitung and built in 1906, a villa-like complex of buildings in the Wallingford district has been given new life as a center for over 20 nonprofit community organizations. Originally built as the Home of the Good Shepherd, it served for over six decades as a place for young women needing shelter, education, and training.

After the home closed in the early 1970s the site was proposed for a shopping center. Thankfully, intense community opposition squelched that idea, and the city purchased the property. The buildings were transferred to Historic Seattle, which set to work converting it to community use.

The grounds surrounding the center contribute as much to its character as the architecture. Some parts resemble small Parisian parks, with regularly spaced trees and quaint benches. There are open, grassy areas and an intimate green flanked by a pavilion and a raised gazebo. There is a formal garden below the rear veranda while a small, almost "secret garden" is to be found off to the side of the main entrance. Two quintessential Seattle touches are a community pea patch and a garden that demonstrates various methods of composting.

Parts of the complex resembles a well-loved ruin: An old brick wall is covered with vines, some planting areas are somewhat mangy and overgrown. A meandering cobblestone path has broken bits of ceramic tile and metal objects worked into its surface. An art piece at the northwest corner, with a stone-encrusted arch and switch-back walkway, gives the sense of entering a special place.

Another project is a dramatic example of how preservation and rehabilitation can help fulfill pressing social needs. Originally built as a "double house" by William Phillips for his family and his parents in 1902, the Heg-Phillips House had seriously deteriorated by the 1980s. In 1992, Historic Seattle purchased the house and set about converting it to 11 units of affordable housing.

Located on the north edge of First Hill, it is a superb example of meticulous renovation. The neo-classical, but asymmetrical, building displays an exquisite ordering of columns, curved bay windows, and a projecting cornice. The building is supremely elegant; it hugs the street edge with an aggressive presence that is unlike most houses in Seattle.

Long before the hospitals got a foothold on First Hill, that part of town was filled with sophisticated homes and apartment buildings. A very few, like the Heg-Phillips House, still exist as a reminder of that era.

Architects Stickney Murphy Romine PLLC designed the restoration of the Heg-Phillips House into 11 units of low-income housing.

A couple of blocks from the Heg-Phillips are the Belmont-Boylston Houses. Historic Seattle converted six houses into 47 units of low-income housing. The "Bel-Boy," along with the Heg-Phillips, offer some valuable lessons in how to provide lower cost housing in a way that is both livable and dignified. Design principles similar to those used in these rehabilitation efforts could be applied to new development as well. These two projects also represent a vital role for Historic Seattle to play: rescuing older houses and transforming them into new and needed forms of affordable housing.

Historic Seattle has more than proved its worth to the community and the region. Without it, we would be a considerably less interesting city.

28

From Lowly Industrial to High Technology

For over 80 years, one of the most enduring and quirky landmarks in Seattle has been the City Light Steam Plant. A huge loaf of a building, its towering smoke stacks made it seem like an ocean liner had somehow gotten itself beached on the shore of Lake Union.

The steam plant was a bold symbol of the early 20th century industrial era. Like a fragment from the set of the silent German movie *Metropolis*, it belched white plumes as electricity was manufactured from a bank of enormous steam-driven turbines.

In 1980, the plant was shut down. Nine years later, shortly after it was designated as a historic landmark, the city-owned utility sold it to the Koll Development Company, which intended to transform it into unusual, loft-style condominiums.

Though approval was granted, the company was unable to secure financing. Subsequently a rapidly growing biotechnology firm—ZymoGenetics—decided that the old steam plant would make a fine, if unconventional, location for its research laboratories. Now, the steam plant has an elegant new skin, a dramatic new interior, and a wholly new use. The result is a spectacular blend of historic preservation, knock-your-socks-off interior design, and cutting edge research.

Walking through the building, it is hard to comprehend the extent of its transformation. Twenty-three million pounds of pipes, boilers, generators, turbines, and other material had to be taken out. Floor slabs were removed and new ones put in to meet the needs of the new use. The stacks were also discarded but were eventually replaced with six somewhat smaller stacks, four of

Architects NBBJ and Daly Associates collaborated on the
transformation of this abandoned steam plant into a headquarters for the ZymoGenetics bio-research company.

which serve to vent the lab spaces.

The building actually sits over the water, atop the same 2,000 first-growth
timber piles that were driven into the shoreline to support the steam plant.
Extensive research revealed the piles to be in good condition, so it was not necessary to supplement them.

Just above the piles, the former basement was converted to two levels of
parking. Prior to renovation, this space had held enormous battered walls that
supported machinery above. Now it is open, and airy, and cool; the lake is only
a few feet below.

Administrative offices occupy the first level, along with the lobby, which
functions as a control point. The company in engaged in a highly competitive
business in which a discovery can mean millions of dollars, so security is tight.
But the public can get a glimpse of the lobby and a typical high bay of the
building through a glass-encased vestibule.

Because the building had been publicly owned, the city required some degree of public access. The public can enter the original plant, a Mission-style structure at the south end. This house-like building was built to contain equipment for generating electricity from water that was piped down from the reservoir in Volunteer Park.

There is an espresso bar on the street side and a dining room on the water side. Lining the walls is a display of historic photos depicting the construction of the plant and its flamboyant appearance during its early years. The sloped ceiling of this gracious little room is lined with original fir planks. A broad deck juts out toward Lake Union. The company also constructed a public walkway on the west side of Fairview Avenue North, along the lake.

Into the center of the building, the architects inserted a quirky staircase that changes form as it twists upward. The stair serves a number of purposes. It connects the different floors, offering a faster access than the elevator. It highlights the two phases of the building. It anchors a corridor that was sliced crossways through the structure, visually linking the hillside with the lake. It provides social space for employees; indeed, one generous landing, cantilevered toward the lake, is known as "The Raft." The designers took their inspiration from a metal, spiral stair that had been in the steam plant but was too unsafe to keep.

But this stair is only a part of the ensemble of the central core. In an effort to recall the imagery of the steam plant, the core is "invaded" by large battered walls covered with metallic, lead-colored paint. These walls are, in turn, visually penetrated by copper-colored "pipes"—actually new structural columns. One floor slab pulls back to allow the battered wall to slide down to the lobby. The theatricality of this piece is emphasized by dramatic lighting.

The ZymoGenetics building is a vivid example of how to breathe new life into older buildings that were initially intended for a unique purpose. Both the architects and the company deserve considerable kudos for giving us back this fine landmark.

29

Extending the
Olmsted Legacy

One of the most breathtaking views in North America is from the little, arched stone bridge that spans part of the lake that is located in the southeast corner of Central Park in New York City. In the foreground, there is an exquisite, restful scene of pastoral beauty: a still pool of water, mature oak trees that bend downward, a gently curving pathway, and tall grasses lining the water's edge. Rising up in the background is a collection of enormous, upward thrusting towers, some turreted and capped with fanciful roofs, others modern and austere.

The effect is at once restful and exciting. It represents, in a single composition, the vitality and brashness of the city. This little bridge is frequently the scene of some strong emotional exchange—an embrace, a kiss, an important bit of conversation, or even weeping.

Very few contemporary parks manage to produce this sort of effect in people. Many are restful, to be sure, but do not stir the passions. Far too many are mostly places for organized sports. At some point in the past 80 years or so, we seemed to forget the importance of building pure parks. Despite a 200-year tradition of doing great village greens, esplanades, and park blocks, we became obsessed with programming public spaces with events and activities. The value of spaces that were simply open and green with places to walk and sit seemed to fall by the wayside.

New York City's Central Park was designed by Frederick Law Olmsted in the mid-1800s. Fifty years later, his son and step-son were commissioned by the City of Seattle to design a network of open spaces. Much of their work we now treasure in the form of places like Seward Park and the Washington Park

Arboretum.

The Olmsted Brothers also envisioned a system of grand parks, greenbelts, and boulevards wrapping all the way around Lake Washington. A few pieces of this larger scheme were built, such as Lake Washington Boulevard.

Now, eight decades later, on the Eastside, a number of splendid parks and open spaces fulfill this vision.

The City of Kirkland has created a necklace of small waterfront parks along its portion of Lake Washington. Although some of these are quite small by typical standards, they are immensely popular. On a warm day in the spring or summer, the scene can resemble the Riviera.

In the City of Renton, Gene Coulon Park, north of the Boeing plant, is a long greenbelt that stretches along the waterfront for several miles. It has a sinuous promenade, metal and glass pavilions, and areas for swimming and boating. The scale of the park is quite intimate, broken only by the visual shock of the immense size of the aircraft plant.

A few years ago, the City of Bellevue opened Newcastle Beach Park, south of the East Channel Bridge on I-90. A simple plane of grass upon which sit a group of deftly proportioned pavilions, the park has received kudos from professional organizations.

The crown jewels in this growing network of Eastside parks is a trio of open spaces that surround downtown Bellevue. The close proximity of such significant tracts of green space to intense development is more common in European countries that have had centuries of experience in infusing their cities with exquisite grown places like the Bois de Boulogne in Paris and Hyde Park in London.

The lowering of the level of Lake Washington in the 1920s left many sloughs of peat and muck that, even back then, no one considered to be worth much of anything. On the Seattle side, in what was already a mature city, folks just dumped garbage into them—they were early, very crude landfills.

Until World War II, the communities on the eastern shore of the lake were quite small, and there was little need for landfills. So Mercer Slough remained a boggy inlet. Over the decades, the slough acquired types of vegetation associated with a true wetland. It is now a vast tract of open land, virtually untouched by development.

It might not have been so, however, were it not for the hard work of many people who fought to keep it out of the hands of developers. In the mid-1980s, plans were being drawn up that would have placed office buildings and hotels all around the edges of the slough, on any sliver of land that was even partially dry. This would have encased the green space, making it the private visual domain of a few hundred office workers.

Instead, today, it is a magnificent park, though not in the conventional sense. The City of Bellevue has acquired almost all of the property. Laced throughout it are soft-surfaced walking trails, but not much else that would disturb the unique natural system. It is also possible to paddle a kayak or canoe down the meandering waterway.

A mile or so to the northeast is Wilburton Hill Park. Much of its 80 acres consists of trees, natural vegetation, and paths. But again, this is a park that almost wasn't. Back in the mid-'70s, the city administration was keen on creating a government center on top of the hill. A city hall, a performing arts center, a headquarters for the school district, even at one time a stadium—all were seen as possible pieces of a civic acropolis of sorts.

But some people had a better idea. Put the public buildings in or near the downtown where they belonged, and make Wilburton Hill into a big park. One forward-thinking family, the Shorts, donated their estate to help start the ball rolling.

One can spend very pleasant hours in the botanical gardens that are a part of the Wilburton Park. The gardens have a large array of plants, some in natural surroundings, some in expertly groomed beds. On one warm Sunday afternoon, a jazz quartet played on the porch of the former Shorts house, which has been transformed into a park pavilion.

Finally, the third member of the trio is the Downtown Park, a place in need of a more romantic name. This park is also the product of heroic efforts by the city and citizens to promote a grand vision and see it through to completion, despite formidable obstacles.

This 17-acre parcel had been owned by the Bellevue School District. Back in the early '80s, the district saw that it owned a potential cash cow. Towers were rising a few blocks away. Property values were in the process of tripling. What better but to lease out the land to people who would throw up 20-story towers. So lucrative did this prospect seem that the district was even willing to donate half of the land to the city for a park.

However, city council members decided that they didn't want just half of it for a park, they wanted *all* of it. And they put their money where their mouth was by issuing bonds to buy the property for a hefty $15 million.

Some citizens came unglued. A public vote was demanded. The city had never in its history bought anything with this kind of sticker price. But the council held fast. Political pressure kept them from spending anything more, however. An attempt to get voter approval to build a park through a park bond election was unsuccessful. The city then issued an announcement: "We picked up some nice property for a park. If anyone out there would care to build it, it's O.K. by us."

Incredibly, someone did. A lot of people, in fact. Several corporations put together a nonprofit foundation that pulled in several million dollars worth of donations from school children to bankers. They then leased the park from the city for a year or so to build it, and turned the key back to the city.

This park is remarkable in that it draws from a tradition of landscape architecture rarely seen in the Pacific Northwest. For whatever reasons, the design of our parks and open spaces has drawn heavily from the English "country garden" school. This suggests a more "natural" appearance, with loose, informal arrangements of vegetation, paths, and structures.

Bellevue's Downtown Park draws from another, equally valid, tradition: the work of Andre Le Notre and other designers in France during the 18th century. In that approach, open spaces are formal, symmetrical, geometric, and have obvious elements of composition. Hard surfaces and objects are used to frame or "mark" spaces.

Mark Hinshaw

Bellevue's downtown park has provided a dramatic focal point to that city's rapidly changing commercial center.

The Downtown Park has all of these characteristics. There is a circular canal of water, which drops down a few inches every so often to match the slope of the land. The canal is ringed, in turn, by a broad path of crushed granite (of the type used in Parisian parks), which is in turn ringed by a circle of plane trees that alternate with obelisk-shaped light fixtures. The inner portion of the park is an open meadow, punctuated by a cluster of trees near, but not exactly in, its center.

The pure geometry of the scheme established the inner meadow as a "sacred" place, one that no one would ever dare disturb by introducing structures or paths. The sole element that is structural is the line of the foundation of the old school building that used to be there—a way of commemorating history when it cannot actually be saved. During midday, from late spring to early fall, this low-slung wall is lined with people sunning themselves.

This is a park that is simply a fine, elegant civic space. No "recreational facilities" mar its appearance or dominate its use. Regardless, people find a wide array of things to do: strolling, jogging, picnicking, sunbathing, wading in the pool, reading on wooden benches. The park has also been used for major civic

Architects Beckley/Myers designed a shallow canal that encircles the downtown park and recalls the proximity of the city to bodies of water.

Mark Hinshaw

festivals. At times it resembles the pointillist painting by Georges Seurat, "Sunday Afternoon on the Grand Jatte." All that is missing is the Victorian dress.

All of these parks and open spaces suggest that the communities around Lake Washington are finally emerging as true cities. One unfortunate hallmark of the postwar suburban era was lack of a "public realm." Suburbs have seemed to be based on notions of exclusivity and private space. Democracy, on the other hand, absolutely depends upon public spaces, inclusiveness, and a collective sense of social responsibility.

This was the very philosophical underpinning of the work by the Olmsteds—the father as well as the sons. I am sure that if they were alive today, and were able to see the evolution of their ideas, they would be very, very pleased.

30

Seattle Center:
The City's Living Room

In October of 1995, the citizens of Seattle presented a huge love note to the people of Puget Sound. A new Seattle Center was revealed in the form of new and renovated buildings, grounds, and fountains. Formerly a tired, somewhat tawdry remnant of the 1962 World's Fair, the place is now absolutely spectacular.

Back in the mid-1980s, Seattle Center was on the verge of being redone by Disney—a completely misguided idea. Instead of a splendid, homegrown regional center, we would have gotten an embarrassingly contrived theme park. Thankfully, the rodent "imagineers" were sent packing.

Subsequently, in 1991, Seattle voters passed a bond issue to improve the center, despite the fact that it is clearly a regional attraction. To this pot was added $83 million of other city money. Another $7.5 million came from the county and

Courtesy of Mahlum Architects

The Charlotte Martin Children's Theatre, designed by Mahlum Architects, is a lively, colorful landmark at one of the entrances to Seattle Center.

state, and $38 million was contributed by the private sector. Clearly, the money has been well-spent.

After decades of a fortress-like appearance along Denny Way, the walls have come down. The Pacific Science Center has a sparkling new facade. All of the inward-facing chintzy pavilion buildings left over from the fair, along with the tired and tacky carnival rides, have been removed from the area around the base of the Space Needle.

The new Charlotte Martin Children's Theatre is one of the most elegant new theaters in the Pacific Northwest. Its artfully articulated front frames a promenade that sweeps in from the west, along the axis of Thomas Street. Usually, a theater's stage house is austere and imposing. This one is like a delicate tapestry.

Designed by NBBJ, the new Key Arena provides a dramatic venue for the Seattle Supersonics and a wide variety of sports and entertainment events.

Perhaps the most dramatic transformation is found in the Key Arena. Previously a structure that managed to combine both dowdiness and kitsch, the former Coliseum is a wonder. The architects essentially designed a wholly new building inside of the old one. The Buck Rogers space station motif has been replaced by well-proportioned forms and details that suggest a lighted pagoda. Formerly awkward spaces around the "legs" of the swooping roof are now generously sized, scalloped public spaces that are both gracious and intimate.

Another "rediscovered" building is the Center House. Originally an armory, its muscular steel roof trusses have been revealed after years of being obscured by a false and flimsy fabric ceiling. The redesign brings loads of natural light into the space from south-facing windows and skylights.

A new entrance court, embellished with fanciful figures by artist Timothy Siciliano, provides a dramatic backdrop to the bosk of mature London plane trees that flank the south side.

At the north end of the Center, the space between the Opera House and Intiman Theatre (known as Founder's Court) has been thoroughly reinvigorated. Previously a rather boring plaza, the area is now more like a private garden.

*Landscape architects Nakano •
Dennis designed improvements to
the International Fountain, which,
together with the Space Needle, is a
landmark within Seattle Center.*

The rather static piece of contemporary sculpture that used to mark the center of this area has been relocated to a more appropriate spot off to the side. A new, quite fascinating, but oddly diminutive fountain has become the focus of attention. Unfortunately, the circular swirling water invites an immediate comparison to a dentist's spitting bowl or another hygienic device of even less social stature.

Finally, the International Fountain in the center of the Center has never been better. It is surrounded by a combination of sloping grass and finely detailed paving. The fountain is animated and surprising. With its acrobatic jets and steam, it appears at times like exploding fireworks.

Seattle Center is clearly in good hands. With strong direction by a variety of organizations and institutions, not to speak of the passionate and driven zeal of director Virginia Anderson, Seattle Center has come alive. It is fun. It is lively. Like a fine old piece of familiar furniture that has been lovingly restored and embellished, the place simply shines.

31

On the Waterfront: The Bell Street Pier

Sydney, Australia, shares many characteristics with Seattle. That dynamic port city on the other side of the Pacific Rim has a skyline bursting with gleaming towers that hug the edge of a spectacular waterfront. A well-preserved historic district is a stone's throw from the "Circular Quay" containing a cruise ship terminal, a fleet of ferry boats that glide across the inlet, and a sinuous esplanade filled with strollers.

Sydney has a monorail that circles around downtown and has a spiky needle complete with the requisite revolving restaurant. The waterfront is even lined with a multilevel viaduct—although Sydney's structural behemoth carries not cars but sleek subway trains.

Several years ago, Sydney completed Darling Harbour, a huge crescent of public spaces, shops, hotels, housing, museums, and meeting facilities. The scale and grandeur of the harbor is enormous; it is virtually a city within the city. A few blocks away, there is a public market that bustles with the business of selling fruit, fish, and vegetables.

Seattle now has a similarly impressive public project on its central waterfront. Put together by the Port of Seattle, the Bell Street Pier complex provides an array of attractions for both locals and visitors. Following close on the heels of its recently completed and exquisitely designed headquarters a few piers to the north, this new development was carefully designed to reflect its place in the city and the region.

That such an extraordinary project could have been done at all in this era of timid government agencies, diminished dollars, and public opposition to almost anything is amazing. Suffice it to say that much of the credit goes to

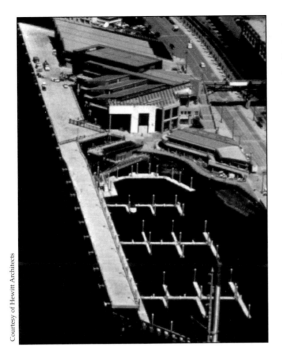

Designed by Hewitt Architects, the Bell Street Pier complex seems like an assemblage of the former cannery structures found along the shores of Puget Sound.

Courtesy of Hewitt Architects

port commissioners who promoted the project as a long-term investment in global trade, and as a "front door" to the city.

From a distance, the Bell Street Pier looks like a compact collection of color-ful metal sheds that might have been progressively plunked down helter skel-ter along the water's edge. This was entirely intended on the part of the designers, drawing from the quirky industrial accretions that grow, barnacle-like, along many urban waterfronts.

But upon closer inspection, the individual parts and pieces are artfully arranged and delicately detailed to offer a setting that is at the same time refined and rough. When the huge cruise ships appear, along with the fishing trawlers, the pier bursts into life, a merger of maritime commerce with urban recreation.

The new short-stay marina has been discovered. Its berths fill up with boats visiting from other places around the world. Patterned after the marina in Victoria, B.C.'s, inner harbor, this protected moorage presents a fine welcome mat to Seattle. The end of the breakwater is marked with a fantastical column by New York artist R.M. Fischer.

Local artist Ann Gardner was commissioned to create a piece that helps shape the central plaza along Alaskan Way. A serpentine wall displaying an intricate mosaic pattern, it forms a lively backdrop to the public "stage" in the center. Opposite the wall, the Odyssey Maritime Museum houses interactive exhibits.

Michael Shopenn

The architecture of the Bell Street Pier displays sophisticated detailing using industrial forms and materials.

Further toward the water is a small, precious fountain in the form of a flopping fish. It is entirely expected that kids will want to wade into its shallow, swirling pool. This energetic water feature was designed by landscape architect Kris Snider, who was inspired by his five-year-old son, Drew.

Although the pier itself is intended for use by passenger ships and trawlers, people can walk right up to the water's edge via a space that is separated from the heavy-duty marine activity by a clever arrangement of sliding gates. There are magnificent views both from the public spaces that swirl around the complex and from raised levels of the building that houses Anthony's Home Port restaurant.

Of all the public spaces, the most dramatic is that perched atop the main building. Accessible by a grand staircase and elevators from Alaskan Way, this deck offers a jaw-dropping 360-degree view of Elliott Bay, the Olympic Mountains, and the stalagmite-like towers of downtown. This public space is at the same elevation as the intersection of Bell Street as it intersects with Elliott Avenue. It can be reached directly from Belltown via a two-level pedestrian bridge, seemingly assembled out of Tinkertoy parts, that dramatically spans Alaskan Way and the train tracks below.

Another access point from downtown is the Lenora Street bridge, a combination of the former concrete viaduct and a new elevator and stair tower. Port

Commissioner Paige Miller points out that these two bridges offer the first handicapped-accessible routes directly from downtown to the waterfront.

The place is superb. And it continues to expand and add new parts. The project included the building of wide sidewalks and decorative street lighting along Alaskan Way over a stretch that has been pretty rough and unattractive. Shops selling products associated with maritime activity will line the street.

On the east side of Alaskan Way, another part of the project is Waterfront Landings, a complex of condominiums. A series of similar, but varied residential buildings are wrapped around quiet courtyards. Located downhill from Pike Place Market, this development further demonstrates how quickly downtown is becoming a desirable place to live.

The best thing about the Bell Street Pier is that it perfectly fits this city. It is elegant but not ostentatious. It is more gangly than grand. It feels like it belongs here and nowhere else.

32

Centering Communities

A short distance south of Boeing Field, the Duwamish River goes through a radical personality change. Suddenly, its angular, hard-edged alignment makes a couple of hairpin turns and all the heavy industry vanishes. The sinuous waterway, its banks lined with thick brush, boat houses, and the back yards of houses, looks like it could be somewhere in rural Tennessee.

The river twists through a tiny neighborhood in the City of Tukwila called Allentown that is filled with diminutive houses on narrow, tree-lined streets. At the south end of this little known hamlet, the Duwamish makes another sharp turn. Perched on the edge is one of the most dramatic and sophisticated community centers in the entire Puget Sound region.

At almost 50,000 square feet, the Tukwila Community Center is surely one of the largest as well. It resembles a city hall or civic center. Indeed, for the people who live and work in Tukwila, the place is rapidly becoming the social center of the community.

The community dates back to the turn of the century and aspects are reflected in the center. As a center of agricultural commerce, Tukwila used to be dotted with distinctively shaped barns and Victorian homes. A few of these remnants actually still remain, buried amidst the tangle of highways and hotels.

Though not literally a barn, the building is composed of forms, details, and materials that make reference to various agrarian structures. The focus of the complex is a huge rotunda, capped by a conical metal roof. Although loosely suggestive of a silo, this is no utilitarian structure. Rather, it is a grand, hotel-like lobby. Large windows ringing the room fill the space with sunlight and permit views of the river and surrounding terrain.

Art has been integrated into this central space in several ways. Artist Michael Kennedy composed a symbolic "River of Life," a meandering visual watercourse set into the ground plane. The piece begins in the front plaza, pen-

Courtesy of ARC Architects

ARC Architects designed this community center both to project a civic presence and to reflect the community's agrarian past.

etrates the interior of the building, and winds out across the riverfront esplanade. In addition there are decorative blocks imprinted with salmon placed on each of the columns around the interior of the rotunda.

Two long, generously wide corridors extend from the rotunda space. One corridor leads to the active recreation spaces, including a large gymnasium, exercise rooms, locker rooms, handball courts, and exterior play fields. The gym is a Spartan, almost industrial space, with exposed steel trusses and a corrugated metal ceiling. Gymnasiums can be somewhat dark and dreary places, but not so here. Huge windows shaded with overhanging wood trellises admit a considerable amount of light into the space.

The other corridor leads to a series of multipurpose rooms, game rooms, dance studios, crafts rooms, and a large and well-appointed senior center. Many of these spaces open out to terraces facing the river. And the rooms are not just generic boxes. They are finished with warm wood on the floors, on ceiling areas, and around windows. Sunlight floods the interior corridor through huge roof monitors that are similar to the cupolas found on rural barns.

Even though the building is one of the largest community centers in the region, its bulk has been visually reduced. The architects cleverly divided the center into small, distinct parts. Projecting bays and an angled arrangement of forms offer an illusion of several buildings grouped tightly together rather than a single, massive one.

The cumulative effect is that the building is friendly and welcoming. The citizens of Tukwila asked for a homey, inviting place and that is precisely what they received.

But the commendable attributes of this community center go beyond the building itself. Parking, arranged in a radiating manner, is laced with planted swales that collect and filter stormwater runoff.

The palette of plants was selected with water conservation in mind. Recycled products, such a compost made from yard waste, were used. The site plan also includes a community demonstration garden for growing vegetables and perennial flowers.

Along the bank of the river, saplings were planted to stabilize the shoreline and create a habitat for fish and wildlife. The network of pathways close to the water's edge provides public access to the water in a way that respects the natural conditions. Grass has been kept to a minimum to reduce the need for fertilizers and herbicides. Instead of the building being surrounded by a useless decorative lawn, there are generous outdoor plaza spaces for community events, celebrations, and socializing.

Much has been written recently about the rising popularity of "third places" that are away from home and work. Some of these places are found in the growing number of coffeebars and cafes. But local governments can add variety to the menu of choices by offering public places like this splendid community center in Tukwila. Such buildings can help both to build a sense of community and to reflect our regional character.

CHAPTER

33

Architecture for Art

Perhaps like many other people in Seattle and Puget Sound, I never considered the Frye Art Museum a major destination. I knew it existed, but not much more. Not what it contained. Not even exactly where it was. Driving through the First Hill neighborhood, I would occasionally get a glimpse of it out of the corner of my eye, make a mental note that I should visit it, and then promptly forget all about it.

The Frye has been around for almost 45 years. It has been open to the public at no charge under terms of the original endowment by Charles and Emma Frye. But it has been somewhat of a hidden treasure.

Some of the Frye's relative obscurity has been due to its being a private museum containing a focused collection of figurative art, essentially the collection of the founders. Additionally, its architecture did not offer much "street appeal." The structure seemed little more than an unadorned concrete warehouse. Even the entrance was not all that welcoming.

When the Frye was originally designed, architects' fascination with the Spartan lines of modern design was reaching its peak. The Frye was not the first museum, nor the last, to find itself housed in a severe box with few external embellishments. To make matters worse, the Frye receded into its site, surrounding itself with a green space of little real use.

But this former wallflower of a museum is no more.

The Frye now has an entirely new image. The architects have teased out of the older edifice a stunning new building that combines dignity with drama. Even the collection looks fresh, hung against rich, dark walls.

The original gallery space was reworked to bring in more natural light from the existing rooftop monitors. The ceilings have been raised, new wood floors have been installed, and the spaces seem lighter and more coherent.

But the boldest moves involve the new additions. A whole new front to the

133

The reconstructed Frye Art Museum, designed by Olsen Sundberg Architects, marks its location with a beacon-like cylindrical entrance.

building was provided along Terry Avenue. A grandly proportioned arcade was positioned right behind the sidewalk, pushing the museum forward toward the street in an aggressive but elegant manner.

The arcade contains a handicapped accessible ramp rising gradually along the length of a reflecting pool. While it is possible to enter the museum more directly from the corner, this is by far the more engaging sequence of approaching the Frye.

Often, a handicapped route to a building is a visually awkward but functional arrangement of ramps leading to the door. Here the passage is entrancing. The columns and roof of the arcade frame a dramatic linear view. Upon entering the arcade, an adjacent reflecting pool is seen at eye level as a smooth, opaque sheet of liquid. At the top of the incline, the building's reflection offers an illusion of depth. A corner of the second floor contains an exquisite composition of metalwork framing the windows.

Between the other vestibule and the lobby are massive bronze doors so finely detailed that they seem like a work of art. In designing these doors and metal screens found elsewhere in the structure, the architects were inspired by the work of Louise Nevelson.

Behind the doors is the main lobby, a cylindrical form capped by a hemisphere that seems to float above your head. This is a space that asks patrons to detach themselves from the world outside and become immersed in the little worlds captured in painting. The otherwise pure geometry of this dome is punctured by an oval that admits soft light into the space. The walls of the cylinder are punctured as well. Two tall, slotted windows afford views of the outside, while other openings offer long vistas of the museum's interior.

The interior of the Frye was transformed from a dreary warehouse to an atmosphere of high drama.

Gregg Krogstad

The control of sunlight is a major challenge in the design of art museums. Too much natural light can detract from and even damage the art. Not enough light can make a museum seem like a tomb. Here light enters through a series of slim windows along one end of the galleries, set perpendicular to the wall within recesses. Through this device, light does not invade the space but gives a soft, subtle presence.

The new Frye contains several more delights. An education wing allows for classes to be given to the public. Large, high-ceilinged studio spaces are designed like industrial lofts. A mechanical system controls the amount of light that enters the work spaces.

The Frye also offers a small cafe that is likely to acquire a following, in part because it offers two very interesting views. One is across the reflecting pool in which the cylindrical form of the lobby is precisely and dramatically reflected.

The other view is into an interior courtyard containing a striking piece of landscape design by Richard Haag. A five-foot-high hemisphere is planted with a blanket of moss, producing the effect of a living geometric form. This mystical object can be seen from the street through a metal screen.

The new Frye is simply smashing. Its elegantly assertive design reaches out to the pubic realm. The reborn Frye Art Museum is a superb addition to the growing number of new and renovated buildings in this region that present visual and performing arts.

34

Splendid Sanctuary

The new Chapel of St. Ignatius at Seattle University is astonishing. Its exquisite sculptural forms transcend mere architecture and manage to elicit the emotional and visceral impact of sculpture.

This is a building that defies conventional notions of geometry, symmetry, and order. Its exterior is disorienting as the eye searches for repetition, right angles, and regularity. Curving roof forms soar off in different directions. Lines that seem to be parallel are not. The thick concrete walls enclosing the structure are composed of many smaller sections fitted together like an enormous, three-dimensional jigsaw puzzle.

On several occasions, I have approached the chapel not from its front, which faces south across a broad lawn and quiet reflecting pool, but from its "back side." The tight clutch of arching forms softly echoes the curve where the street turns. Here it is possible to closely inspect the delicate details and fine craftsmanship. The mottled patina of the exterior walls invites the hand to touch. The crisp edges of the zinc sheeting covering the roof are exposed, revealing a light, paper-thin covering on a building that is otherwise chunky and solid.

Six curving and angular shapes protrude upward from the main structure, while a seventh forms the slender bell tower in front. From the outside, windows seem completely haphazard in shape and location, aligning not with each other nor any other part of the building.

Inside the building, these openings admit natural light into major spaces, creating visual effects upon the walls and ceilings that are stunning. Colored panes of glass that form portions of skylights cast hues that softly infuse different sections of the interior with a warm glow. Some of these swatches of light seem to be produced if by magic; their source is not immediately apparent. Some of the colors are produced by direct light and others are reflected, an effect that is mysterious and mystifying.

The St. Ignatius Chapel at Seattle University serves as a luminscent lantern, creating an ethereal architectural object. Architect Steven Holl, with the assistance of Olsen Sundberg Architects, created the design.

One of the most dazzling effects is found at the back of the choir alcove. Looking up, one sees what seems to be a rectangle of red so intense that is burns an image on the back of the retina. Staring into this window is mesmerizing, creating a sensation of being lifted from the floor. Few contemporary buildings mange to manipulate natural light in such a spectacular manner.

Next to the choir is a small room, the Blessed Sacrament Chapel, that is also filled with a warm glow. Artist Linda Beaumont embellished this space, coating its walls with shiny beeswax. The room is both intimate and precious. Her stunning arrangement of a large madrona branch, together with sacred symbols and prayers, reflects a religion with a rich past.

Deeply held traditions are also embodied in the main sanctuary. Arched forms suggest ancient vaulted churches. The building seems as if it might have been made several centuries ago. Walls curve into ceilings, as if constructed stone by stone.

In comparison with many modern buildings that lose their appeal with extended viewing, this one gets more rewarding. A slight shift in vantage point sets up a different combination of deep, light-filled slots and sinuous shapes. The complexity of the space and the ethereal play of light are offset by walls that are almost crude in appearance. With their simple, roughly finished surfaces, they seem almost like sack cloth.

Virtually everything in the building is one of a kind. Glass light fixtures suspended in the main sanctuary resemble delicate soap bubbles that have just burst. Door pulls and ventilation grilles made of cast bronze add richness and depth. The interior spaces and fittings convey a striking combination of roughness and precision.

For example, the tiny, cistern-like confessional room is accessed by pulling open a delicately balanced, L-shaped door the size of a wall. Of polished, blond wood, the door is surrounded by rough plaster. It is suggestive of a box filled with secrets, which, in fact, it is. The skylight covering the room projects a patch of orange light that slowly travels across the surfaces as the sun moves.

This is a building that sharpens the senses as it touches the soul.

VI

Public Works as Public Art

Sometime in the years following World War II, engineers took over community development. Perhaps this came out of the war: Science and technology had, after all, put a stop to a dark era and propelled us into prosperity. But the outcome, over time, has been a host of completely utilitarian, mean, and soulless places.

Our neighborhoods are now sliced apart by broad corridors of concrete and asphalt, with no criteria except the flow of vehicles—like water through a pipe—being considered. Bridges and highways are austere structures trimmed back to their essential, load-bearing purposes. Some even resemble engineering diagrams in their simplistic forms. Waterways have been channeled for efficiency, their banks stripped of vegetation. Almost all of the parts of our street environment, which used to have charming street lights, trees, and other decorative elements, have been replaced with standardized steel fixtures selected from catalogs and conforming to engineering manuals. We now have entire neighborhoods, streets, and districts that are completely devoid of anything that would touch the human heart.

Fortunately Seattle saw this coming and started a counter-movement. In the early 1970s, it set up the first public arts commission. Although Washington, D.C.'s Fine Arts Commission predated the Seattle Arts Commission, the charge of the former was much broader. SAC was to focus solely on commissioning and curating a collection of art to be located in public places. In the subsequent 25 years, hundreds of works of art have been purchased. These are found in parks, plazas, along streets, in libraries, in community centers, in neighborhoods, downtown, in city hall, even at power stations and reservoirs.

This spawned two groups of people: those who want more of it and those who produce it. Citistate Seattle now has, outside of New York City, one of the greatest concentrations of artists in the country. The culture has created a sup-

Columns designed to look like seaweed and barnacle-encrusted piers by Nancy Hammer flank the grand entry stairs in the Port of Seattle headquarters.

portive climate for visual artists, playwrights, writers, musicians, actors, dancers, and choreographers. There are at least a dozen, permanent, "mainstream" theater groups and several dozen alternative groups. Citistate Seattle has a half dozen art museums and scores of art galleries. Corporations and governments alike contribute to the arts, knowing that they are not a frill but a necessity.

As this environment flourishes, we are now seeing the real fruits—a whole host of truly extraordinary works. Public art now blends visual form, sculpture, architecture, and the landscape. The result suffuses the culture of Citistate Seattle.

35

Waterworks

During the last several years, public agencies have been engaged in various forms of what is known as environmental "remediation." Toxic waste sites are being cleaned up. Deforested areas are being replanted. And deteriorated streams and lakes are being brought back to support fish and wildlife.

Sometimes, however, efforts in this vein produce their own negative impacts. Innumerable neighborhoods have been inflicted with the ugly sites of former service stations, their lots surrounded by "temporary" chain link fencing and covered with black asphalt or plastic sheeting. Apparently, no thought was given to the fact that, while the site was being repaired, people continue to live nearby.

The enormous concrete walls recently installed on our freeways are another case in point. With a narrow, single-minded objective of reducing noise for homes, highway engineers have erected miles of austere structures that are about as charming as a penal institution. Only strands of razor wire would be needed to complete the look. This did not need to be so insensitively done. Similar walls constructed elsewhere in the country have been gracefully designed, sometimes incorporating the work of artists.

Finally, in their zeal to control and cleanse stormwater runoff, regulatory agencies have been requiring that development projects build huge sloping pits, called "bio-swales," that are planted with grasses and occasionally hold water. No matter that this damp, rolling terrain is virtually impassable by people on foot. No matter that otherwise connected land uses are fractured by the man-made streams and rendered useless for any other activity. No, the single objective of repairing environmental damage seems to take precedence over all other social purposes.

That is why it is so remarkable to witness the rare circumstance in which a multitude of objectives are respected and accommodated. Such is to be found

Waterworks Gardens is both a work of art and a functioning system for cleaning stormwater runoff. Artist Lorna Jordan created a unique blend of art and landscape.

at Waterworks Gardens, located at the north edge of the King County Sewage Treatment Plant in Renton. At the southeast corner of Monster Road and Oakdale is an astonishing place—one that serves an important environmental function, that is a vivid demonstration of enlightened remediation techniques, and that presents itself as a captivating work of art.

Waterworks was designed by an artist. Selected by the Metro Arts Committee, Lorna Jordan was assigned the task of doing something with what had been planned to be a series of open, detention ponds to catch and clean the stormwater produced by the sprawling plant. She was teamed with an engineering firm, which was charged with making the installation function properly.

Jordan might have played a more typical artist's role of placing objects about the landscape but leaving the essential layout and organization to the engineers. Instead, she jumped in and immediately started pressing for a fundamentally different way of locating, configuring, and embellishing the ponds.

Jordan designed the entry portion to be an overlook marked by dramatic, rough stone columns. Water is visible and audible beneath a meandering metal grate.

Lorna Jordan

People strolling through the Waterworks discover this mysterious grotto that is cool, serene, and lined with mosaic tiles.

But, because this would require a great deal of technical expertise and experimentation, she conducted an exhaustive research effort into what was being done creatively elsewhere in the country.

The design process was completely collaborative. There was a willingness among all participants to break the conventional rules and try something different. Ideas flowed freely and professional boundaries were blurred. People within various agencies were willing to take major risks, rather than merely following manuals. Everyone viewed this project from the perspective of not merely solving problems but creating opportunities.

What emerged and was ultimately built is a diverse and thoroughly enjoyable public place. No chain link surrounds the eight-acre site. Pathways invite people to walk in from several directions. There is a direct connection with the City of Renton's trail along Springbrook Creek. Neither huge signs nor tall lights mar this serene and verdant environment.

Jordan's design arranges the various bodies of water in a composition that roughly resembles a plant pulled from the ground and laid on its side. The uppermost pond is surrounded by the "roots," represented by a set of crude stone columns. They enclose a walking surface of cobblestones, stone slabs, and industrial steel grating beneath which rushing water can be seen and heard. The effect is both highly tactile and vaguely archaeological, as if one happened upon ancient ruins.

From a handrail-lined platform on the edge of the first open pond, it is possible to overlook the entire piece and see its furthest point. That distant spot, near a vehicular bridge that crosses Springbrook Creek, is where the water has been finally made sufficiently clean to enter the regional waterways. Several sinuously curved linear ponds, filled with thick grasses, converge at that point. This is the head of the plant and the setting is already sufficiently restored to support an abundance of small animals, waterfowl, and songbirds.

The ponds located between the highest pond and the lowest pond step gradually down the hillside in a series of terraces. A curving pathway serves as the main "trunk" of the plant. Halfway along its length is a semi-enclosed space that feels like a huge seed pod that seemingly has just burst open. Jordan calls this the Grotto, a place shaped with high curving walls lined with ferns and shade plants. Ceramic tiles on the floor of the grotto and on the sitting ledges create a sense of mystery. A small, crude fountain infuses the place with a cool humidity and the soothing sound of water over rock.

Waterworks Gardens is a completely unexpected and thoroughly engaging blend of technology and artistry. It combines symbolism with a practical function, public works with public access. It educates as it entertains. As Jordan puts it, "It speaks to both nature and culture."

As a work of public art, Waterworks Gardens is rich and rewarding. As a public works project, it is amazing.

36

The Port as a
Patron of the Arts

North American waterfronts have not been known for their wonderful architecture. Until the last 10 years, they have been either grungy, even derelict, industrial areas or places lined with T-shirt shops and trinket-selling enterprises aimed mainly at the tourist trade.

Fifteen years ago, Boston transformed its waterfront into a lively, elegant public place by renovating several piers, providing an esplanade, and encouraging bold new buildings such as Rowes Wharf with its grand archway. Baltimore has received international acclaim for its Inner Harbor development of pubic spaces, civic buildings, fine restaurants, and upscale shops. More recently, Washington Harbor in Washington, D.C., has created a place where people can stroll along the Potomac, weaving through fountains and outdoor cafes packed into the late evening.

Seattle has been a bit tardy in this regard. Though its waterfront bustles with commuters around the Ferry Terminal and it has a fine aquarium, much of the place has little to offer people who live here. I always feel a bit awkward among the hordes of people in shorts and loud shirts streaming along Alaskan Way. There are few places that seem comfortable enough for quite contemplation of the bay.

But things are changing. The Port of Seattle has been completing an ambitious plan to connect the waterfront to the uplands, to introduce fine public buildings, and to infuse the area with new housing and hotels. Along with this is a continuous promenade on the east side of Alaskan Way, allowing a choice away from the honky tonk and hawking. This is one of the best public buildings we have seen in this city in a long time—most certainly in the downtown.

Architects Hewitt Isley transformed old Pier 69 into a stunning new headquarters for the Port of Seattle.

The building is big. At 300,000 square feet and 750 feet long, it is virtually like a high rise tower laid on its side. But, unlike many large buildings, this one seems to present a different face from every angle, as it responds to different conditions around it.

The south facade is taut and flush, broken only slightly by bracketed overhangs that provide shade for long rows of punched windows. Clearly, the reference is to the pattern of sleek metal and glass found on luxury ocean liners.

The east face thrusts itself upon the street with a combination of dignity and whimsy. The "prow" of the upper floor is punctured to reveal that the facade is almost paper thin—the cantilevered form is as bold as it is light. The broad entry steps seem a bit sterile though; something more might have been done here to engage passersby.

The north facade reveals the original concrete columns supporting the massive structure with indentations that produce an industrial looking bay window. Along the ground a series of painted footprints lead people to the end of the pier where one can find a quiet place to look across the water.

It is not widely known that this building, being public, allows for access into much of its interior. By merely requesting a visitor's badge at the desk it is easy to walk into the long, high-ceiling interior atrium on the second floor. This trip is well worth the effort, as the building is chock full of splendid pieces of art and the most mystical interior spaces in the city.

Patrick Barta

The dramatic, multistory atrium is filled with light. A sinuous water feature, designed by landscape architect Bob Murase, evokes the importance of water to the region.

Directly behind the reception desk is a grand staircase flanked by columns created by artist Nancy Hammer. Encrusted by swirling seaweed shapes and glistening glazed tiles, the effect is akin to entering an undersea grotto. Down behind the stair is the Portside Cafe—also open to the public —that offers fine, reasonably priced lunchtime fare in elegant surroundings with a view of the water.

But back to the grand staircase. Reaching the top, one discovers what is in a sense a "secret garden." But no plants are in sight, just rocks and water. But what a rock garden this is. A long, sinuous, shallow stream follows the length of the space, accentuating its linear form. It is lined with sharply honed shapes of granite that convey a sense of mystery.

It is possible to accidentally step into the watercourse, so it is necessary to pay attention. The water makes a soft, soothing sound as it emerges from the rocks and moves along the space. There is a sense of entering ancient ceremonial chambers. The larger room is connected to a smaller room, which eventually leads out to a small balcony that overlooks the bay.

The progression of water and stonework offers a magnificent sense of serenity. Though people can be seen all around, the space seems private and contemplative. This weaving of architecture, art, and craftsmanship is exceptional. Public buildings have rarely been as splendid.

37

Buildings for Books

Over the past couple of years, the King County Library System has opened new and expanded structures that were funded by a $67 million bond issue approved by voters of the district in 1988. To its credit, the county system did not try to develop a generic building type and then repeat it endlessly. Instead, each library is the result of a unique design effort, blending the talents of many fine local architects, criteria set forth by the district, and desires of the surrounding community.

These are not demure little havens tucked into the woods. They are assertive, imaginative, sophisticated, and urbane. They are landmarks in their own right, lending both dignity and verve to the function they serve.

Like many people, I have a deep-rooted fascination and respect for libraries. As a child in Minneapolis, I would hop a city bus on Saturday mornings and find myself a half hour later buried amidst the stacks. Fingering those little bits of paper in the polished wooden trays of the catalog files would always invoke a sense of imminent discovery.

An argument can easily be made that libraries are our most important public buildings. They encourage reading—that most vital of skills. They are repositories of information and ideas, wit and wisdom, literature and legend. They are living, working symbols of our culture and our civilization.

Library architecture can itself be inspiring. Just approaching the great cascading steps of the New York Public Library is an adventure. Even the wonderful little Carnegie libraries, many of which are still around, instill a sense of awe.

Unfortunately, for much of the last three or four decades, library architecture suffered from a mean-spirited aesthetic driven by bureaucrats and boards bent more on warehousing book collections than celebrating them. Thankfully that era has come to an end.

Cities across North America have recently opened new or expanded libraries, some with world class architecture. The new library in Chicago, with its neo-classical design, is a great addition to the Loop. Vancouver, B.C.'s recently opened downtown library, with its allusions to the Roman coliseum, is breathtaking. The boldly scaled geometric forms of the new library in Denver give it a fantastical image.

Within Washington State, both Everett and Spokane recently remodeled or built new libraries within their downtowns. King County's regional headquarters library in downtown Bellevue set in motion a trend toward fine civic structures previously unseen on the Eastside.

ZGF Architects created a new landmark for downtown Kirkland.

The new library in downtown Kirkland creates a spectacular gatehouse to one corner of Peter Kirk Park. Two decades of building up its central core into a tight-knit, mixed use district has borne fruit in the creation of an exquisite, finely detailed piece of public architecture.

The library in downtown Bothell seems to belong to the same family as the buildings in Bellevue and Kirkland. Its dramatic curved roof and brick walls speak of a permanence and public realm that has been missing in that community. Too bad it was not made a part of a true civic center.

Similarly, the library on 175th Street in Shoreline is a prominent piece of work that should provide a sense of pride to that recently incorporated community. Both the library in Woodinville and the one in Covington on the outskirts of Kent are less deftly detailed but nonetheless are statements about what libraries can do for otherwise nondescript areas.

The library district decided to fund the addition of art into these buildings, even though it had no legal requirement to do so. Many fine pieces have been commissioned for lobbies and forecourts that enhance the experience of entering the buildings. In some cases, artists were treated—as they should be—as a part of the design team and fashioned elements like lighting fixtures.

The trouble with many of these buildings is that, as fine as they are, they deserve to be part of a grander vision, one that combines open space, pedestrian connections, and other community functions. It is truly unfortunate, for example, that the Woodinville library is not even within the city limits. It should have been a part of the emerging city center area.

The Bothell library is so closely surrounded by the clutter of strip malls, car washes, and gas stations that it is scarcely visible from any major street. And, for the life of me, I cannot imagine why the Federal Way Library was made to look like a cubist jack-o'-lantern. What were they thinking?

But even with these shortcomings, the new libraries found throughout King County are a fine testament to what local government can do when let loose by the electorate. It is also a taste of what we can get when we look beyond the boundaries of purely local interests.

38

Learning From Tukwila

My high school was not unlike a medium security prison. A collection of flat-roofed boxes almost devoid of windows, it sat in the center of a vast tract of land. An expansive apron of asphalt lay between the street and the front doors. Around the perimeter was a "clear zone" containing few trees that might conceal someone attempting to escape the confines of the compound.

Most high schools built during the past 30 years have followed this formula. The idea of a school as a free-standing, isolated building has held sway with school administrators and architects. Throughout the country we now have hundreds of schools that are cut off from their surroundings. They project an image of incarceration more than of participation in learning and community life.

Fortunately for us in Puget Sound, there is a new high school that demonstrates another approach. Tucked within the interior of Tukwila, a stone's throw from Highway 99, is the new Foster High School. It is one of the most sophisticated and urbane high schools seen in these parts in a long, long time.

Built on the site of its '50s-era predecessor, Foster High manages to pull off, through its design, a number of quite stunning accomplishments.

The school is a true civic building both in its use and as a symbol. The architects did not follow the conventional pattern of austere and isolated school buildings. Instead, they drew from a much deeper and richer tradition. This is the tradition of the grand and dignified school buildings that were constructed during the first several decades of this century, many of which still stand today.

Foster High School does not recede; it commands attention with a bold, but graceful, face. The sides facing the adjacent street are elegant compositions of brick and generous windows. Each of the two wings of the school is capped by a visually strong, double-pitched metal roof. A decorative frieze of colored

Designed by BJSS Architects, the new Foster High School recalls the solid, classic educational buildings of 70 to 80 years ago.

ceramic tiles dances along the cornice line.

Each wing of the school is pushed up toward the street, rather than away from it. The buildings are parallel to the intersecting streets and dramatically anchor the corner. Here, at last, is a school that places its parking *behind* the buildings. Contributing to the image of the community was clearly seen as a more important objective than conveying the presence of parking.

Foster High School is much more than a school. It is a community center. Much lip service has been given to the use of schools for community activities. This is one that encourages community use in a major way. The school includes a 500-seat performing arts theater. It is fully equipped with a fly loft, wing space, dressing rooms, sound and lighting systems, and comfortable seats. (The City of Tukwila provided funds to obtain some of these features.) The theater is not buried in the bowels of the school. Rather, it is in a highly visible, central location and has its own architectural expression. The theater is available for public events and theatrical productions.

Moreover, the "commons room" in the school is frequently used for community meetings. And classrooms are booked for adult education classes and seminars in the evening. The design seems to invite use by the public.

The school is arranged around an open public space that is visible from the streets. This space seems a bit stiff and barren. As nearby planting matures, however, the space might become more appealing. The school district should consider purchasing a few dozen inexpensive, molded plastic chairs and placing them in the space. People could then arrange them as they wish.

The interior corridors are so generous in size and height as to make the word "hallway" seem inadequate. With their vertical proportions and continuous skylights, these corridors are somewhat reminiscent of the "passages" found throughout the older parts of Paris. Even the floors, covered in terrazzo, are elegant. The materials and finishes throughout the school are of a quality that demands respect. Indeed, there are no graffiti, or other signs of abuse, even in out-of-sight restrooms. This is especially remarkable since the school has a relatively transient student body. Every year, one-third of the students move. In addition, 40 percent come from families with incomes below the poverty level. It is clear that the students care a lot for their school.

The design of Foster High School is sufficiently strong that it can serve as a catalyst for other development in the vicinity. Recently, a new Larry's Market has opened a few blocks away on 99 with a design that, like the school, introduces a level of quality and vitality not previously seen in the area. The King County Library District recently built a new branch library just across the street.

Finally, although the school is filled with finely detailed features, its cost was not at all excessive. To the contrary, the building was constructed at a cost per square foot that was significantly below the average for schools within this state. Enough funds were left over in the budget to enable the school administration to buy state-of-the-art equipment and fixtures. Foster High School is a dramatic demonstration that good design need not cost more.

39

Art in Transit

Sometime in the years that followed World War II, the design of our public transportation systems—our streets and sidewalks, our buses and trains, our highways and ferryboats—were taken over by people with a very narrow perspective. Objectives of operational efficiency, low maintenance, inexpensive materials, and austere aesthetics overshadowed every other design criteria.

Now, after more than 50 years of this dominant mentality we can see the results in places and objects all around us that are visually impoverished, devoid of any embellishing details that bring joy and enrichment to our daily lives. Overly wide asphalt streets, stripped of trees that were once a hallmark of gracious city living, plunge relentlessly through neighborhoods and business districts. Lighting fixtures now come out of a catalog, with the choices ranging from Spartan to ugly.

Vehicles used in transportation used to exhibit a great deal of charm and careful craft. Think of the old Brill trolley bus with its swept-back, aerodynamic profile. Or the early ferries with their burnished wood trim. Even the labyrinthine and cacophonous New York City subway system was graced with elegantly capped columns along the platforms.

It sometimes seems that in recent decades everything has been designed by numbers, and indeed, that has been the case, Engineering manuals have standardized virtually everything within the public realm in the name of efficiency. Roads and vehicles have been designed almost like pipes: smooth and clean to ensure maximum flow. For example, wherever you go—big city, small town, suburb, or in-town neighborhood —you can see the same "cobra head" light on its plain, galvanized metal pole.

We do not tolerate such an absence of variety and character in any other aspect of our communities. We debate the design of libraries, schools, parks, city halls, and community centers—as we should—to ensure that we get the best possible blending of creativity and cost considerations. But the design of the transportation network rarely has been done in the spotlight of public discourse.

Fortunately, this is beginning to change for us who live in Citistate Seattle. Ten years ago, the designers of the transit tunnel in downtown Seattle showed that art and architecture can humanize and enliven public spaces devoted to moving people and vehicles. The result is a splendid combination of finely joined materials, colors, elegant lighting, subtle signs, and intriguing works of art.

A few years ago, Metro began to rethink the color scheme for its bus fleet. While this effort has been somewhat diverted by a misguided trend to treat buses as moving billboards, we are seeing a growing number of the handsomely painted vehicles. A group of artists and graphic designers collaborated to develop a design that respects the geometry of the bus while infusing it with both style and whimsy.

Other examples have begun to pop up around the region. Bus stops on Rainier Avenue South are peppered with art installations, including wonderfully goofy whirligigs by Carl Smool. Along N.E. Eighth in Bellevue, a series of uniquely designed bus shelters are highlighted by walls incorporating hundreds of decorative tiles designed by school children. And along International Boulevard in the City of Sea Tac, bus shelters hold etched glass panels by artists Lydia Aldredge and Kate Wade.

In downtown Mercer Island, for the main pedestrian and transit street, artist T. Ellen Sollod designed delightful metallic ribbons that swirl around light poles, as well as cast metal images inlaid in the sidewalk. The recently completed reconstruction and expansion of the esplanade along Alki Beach in Seattle includes cast concrete illustrations of local marine life.

By far the most extensive and dramatic recent example of infusing a transportation corridor with art is to be found along the three-mile long Fairview/Eastlake corridor. The entire length, from Denny Way to the University Bridge, is framed with new trolley poles and street lights that have been painted a vivid and unexpected color of turquoise.

Artist Carolyn Law came up with the unifying color scheme for the scores of poles, but painted four at the intersection of Eastlake and Hamlin with different and very striking designs. One pole seems to be covered with glistening fish scales. Another looks as if it were hand-dipped into a succession of different paint buckets. A series of poles along several blocks have pieces of driftwood attached to them. For elements that typically recede into the background, the effect is arresting.

The notion of "art in transit" was more literally interpreted by Law in stringing colored ceramic "beads"—actually standard electrical parts—into the guy wires that hold up the trolley power lines. Calling them "trolley jewelry," she

Artist Ellen Sollod worked with a design team to embellish light fixtures along the downtown streets of Mercer Island.

T. Ellen Sollod

found an ingenious way to enhance the ganglia of unsightly wires that mark so many of Seattle's intersections.

Less successful as an integrated work of art is the series of sailboat-like masts that top a number of the poles on the west side of Fairview Avenue North. Meant to play off of the presence of boats in the many marinas, these objects merely compound the visual clutter of wires and metal poles in the area.

But further up the street, between East Boston and Roanoke streets, are two entirely delightful works of art that address both the context of the specific neighborhood and the experience of movement whether walking, biking, driving, or riding in a bus. The pieces are at once simple and complex. Even though I see them every day, there seems to be always something that I did not notice before.

The "Dreamboats" are the result of a collaborative group of artists called Stable. Composed of artists Linda Beaumont, Stuart Keeler, and Michael Machnic,

A series of whimsical kiosks evokes the character of the Eastlake neighborhood.

the group created three exquisite pergolas. At first seeming to be slender bus shelters, they are actually commentaries on history, behavior, and lifestyle. Shapes resembling kayaks are upturned and mounted on black metal trestle-like structures. Metal oars undulate rhythmically along the hulls

At night, the boats seem to be made of embossed paper or bark and glow with a muted, ethereal light. Small touches abound for people on foot. Coins have been strewn around one of pergolas next to a bus stop, as if someone lost some pocket change. At another, a serpentine stone seat beckons. But no one seems to have taken up an invitation to post notices on the metal fins of the middle pergola. Possibly, people see the pergolas as too precious.

"Cornerstones" designed by artist Stacy Levy and laid into the sidewalks at numerous intersections display a keen sense of humor. Squares of finely cast concrete contain illustrations of microscopic organisms found in Lake Union. The prickly/squirmy images, with their unpronounceable scientific names, make you smile as you feel an irresistible itch. The colored glass bricks set next to these depictions are simply gorgeous. Backed with reflective foil, they emanate a mysterious light that seems to come from deep inside the earth.

The spectacular and engaging infusion of art into the Eastlake corridor proves that we can, indeed, rethink the role that streets have in building communities. Public works can be works of art.

Epilogue

This region, the place I have described as Citistate Seattle, is currently the subject of a grand experiment. We are the first major urban region in modern history to make an attempt to deliberately direct the location, the intensity, and the quality of development, all the while protecting forests and farmlands, wildlife and wetlands—creating a city within a wilderness.

We have taken on the task of ensuring that this part of the world is livable not just for ourselves, but for future generations. And we are not content to make it merely livable, for that would mean little more than maintaining the status quo. Rather, we are determined to make this region, with its dynamic economy and complex ecology, decidedly more complex, more dynamic, more diverse, more humane, more democratic, and more collectively responsible. A more daunting assignment would hardly be possible.

As I write these final words, I am looking out from the roof deck of my houseboat, across the expanse of Lake Union in the heart of the city. Crisscrossing the lake are sailboats and motorboats, kayaks and canoes. Big tour boats glide by, their decks brimming with folks from Korea and Kansas. Overhead, seaplanes shuttle people to distant islands, while passenger jets coast down toward the airport with a fresh load of newcomers. The surface of the water sparkles as the sun glints off of thousands of tiny swells.

Of all the places in the world that I have lived and visited, Seattle is, without a doubt, the most manageable, the most mannerly, and the most magical.

I, for one, intend to do my part to keep it that way.

REFERENCES

Crowley, Walt. *National Trust Guide: Seattle*. New York: John Wiley and Sons, 1998.

Dorpat, Pat. *Seattle Now and Then. 2d ed.* Tartu Publishers, 1990.

Kelbaugh, Doug. *Common Place: Toward Neighborhood & Regional Design*. Seattle: University of Washington Press, 1997.

Kelbaugh, Doug, ed. *Pedestrian Pocket Book: A New Suburban Design Strategy*. New York: Princeton Architectural Press, 1989.

Murray, Morgan. *Skid Row: An Informal Portrait of Seattle*. Seattle: University of Washington Press, 1982.

———. *Puget's Sound: A Narrative of Early Tacoma and the Southern Sound*. Seattle: University of Washington Press, 1981.

Ochsner, Jeffery Karl, ed. *Shaping Seattle Architecture: A Historical Guide to the Architects*. Seattle: University of Washington Press, 1994.

Sales, Roger. *Seattle Past to Present*. Seattle: University of Washington Press, 1978.

Saunders, William, ed. *Richard Haag: Bloedel Reserve & Gasworks Park*. New York: Princeton Architectural Press, 1998.

Shamash, Diane, and Steven Huss. *A Field Guide to Seattle's Public Art*. Seattle: Seattle Arts Commission, 1991.

Wenger, Loralee. *Seattle Access. 3d ed.* New York: Harper Collins, 1997.

Woodbridge, Sally B., and Roger Montgomery. *A Guide to Architecture in Washington State*. Seattle: University of Washington Press, 1980.

INDEX